QUESTIONS
PEOPLE ASK

QUESTIONS
PEOPLE ASK

———— ✧ ————

By Robert J. McCracken

————————

Harper & Brothers

PUBLISHERS NEW YORK

Contents

Foreword

As soon as religion becomes a live issue it poses questions. The questions vary from person to person and from generation to generation. At the deeper levels, however, one is aware of a recurring quality and an essential similarity in the questions people ask. Let a man claim the right to look at things for himself and to form his own judgements and he is certain to put to himself inquiries of the kind that have been raised from the beginning of time, basic inquiries having to do with the existence and character of God, the nature and destiny of man, the relation of man to his Maker and to his fellows. For those for whom such inquiries are urgent as well as significant an easy faith is a contradiction in terms, insulting alike to the intelligence and the conscience. They have to do battle for faith. They possess it only as they recapture it day by day.

These sermons were preached with such people in mind. They represent an attempt to come to grips with the religious and moral difficulties confronting men and women in the modern world, first by facing each difficulty frankly and openly, and then by bringing to bear on it Christian insights and applications. The questions range wide, but a glance at the chapter headings should be sufficient to indicate that they are bona fide questions. In everyday contact with people and, taken into their confidence, these are the problems they have presented.

This, of course, is preaching in only one of its aspects. It is not doctrinal, though doctrine is involved. It is not Biblical, though it

7

would be my contention that Biblical insights are implicit and explicit from start to finish. This is life-situation preaching in which the preacher finds the point of departure in a real, contemporary problem. It may be social or personal; it may be theological or ethical or psychological. Whatever it is, his first business is to get at the core of it, and, that done, to seek as cogently and helpfully as he knows how, to work out the solution, with the mind and spirit of Jesus and the Biblical revelation the constant points of reference and direction. I judge that this is the type of preaching of which there is particular need to-day.

For permission to quote copyrighted material I am indebted to: *The Canadian Baptist* for the poem by May Richstone; The Macmillan Company for the quotation from *The Seekers* by John Masefield; the executors of the estate of the late Sir Henry Newbolt for the quotation from Sailing at Dawn from *Poems Old and New;* Miss Erica Oxenham for the quotations by John Oxenham; Oxford University Press for the quotation from *Sleep of Prisoners* by Christopher Fry; William Sloane, Associates, Inc. for the quotation from *High Tor* by Maxwell Anderson.

In sending this book forth I gratefully acknowledge the debt I owe in respect of its origins to the congregation of the Riverside Church. No man could wish for a pulpit more challenging or for a hearing more stimulating.

ROBERT J. McCRACKEN

QUESTIONS
PEOPLE ASK

How Does One Acquire Religious Experience?

WHEN Dr. R. F. Horton, a notable Congregationalist minister, was at Oxford as an undergraduate he attended T. H. Green's classes in philosophy. In his diary at the time he made this entry: "I attended Green's lectures and came into close personal contact with him. Never can I forget his expression when one day he found that I had a real and vivid faith in Christ. 'You are very fortunate' was his brief, intense comment."

Now Green was an honest and powerful thinker and a great and good man. How did it come about that the instructor lacked the experience that the student enjoyed, an experience that he envied and apparently would have been happy to possess? What gives point to the question is that there are large numbers of people—I have no doubt that there are some here—who are in fundamentally the same position as Green. They have a good mind and a sound character, yet they will tell you that they have no religious experience to speak of; they believe in God, but His bare existence is about all they believe in; they do not have—what Green was quick to notice Horton had—a real and vivid faith.

And sometimes, not having acquired religious experience,

11

they deny that there is any such thing. They are not prepared, they say, to believe in anything of which they have no first-hand acquaintance. "Seeing is believing" is their formula. "Unless," said Thomas, when they told him Jesus had risen, "I see his hands with the mark of the nails, and put my finger where the nails were, I refuse to believe." Even as I quote that I am thinking of a student who tells me that he no longer believes in prayer; he has tried it and has found that it doesn't work. I tell him that his use of the word work makes me wonder whether after all he is familiar with the true nature of prayer, whether he isn't thinking of it as a device like a penny-in-the-slot machine; you put something in and automatically get something out. I tell him that, whatever his subjective state and whatever the immediate result, he should persist with prayer, at the same time pointing out that Bach and Beethoven and Brahms mean infinitely more to him to-day than when his father practically had to bribe him into attending his first symphony concert. And, of course, I remind him of the experience of the saints, apostles, martyrs, prophets in every age. Is all that wealth of cumulative testimony, all that unanimity of conviction to be dismissed out of hand as so much mystical moonshine, as mere wishful thinking? Have all those myriad souls of every nation and kindred and people and tongue been pulling at strings to which nothing was attached? Has Dr. Fosdick stepped into this pulpit Sunday after Sunday, year after year, and at the appointed time for prayer, proceeded to do no more than talk into space? On that premise what a farce worship is, whether public or private!

Observe where, in the case of individual after individual, the weakness of the premise lies. They are not prepared to believe in anything that they themselves have not experienced. But that's absurd. To refuse to admit a fact simply and solely on the ground that it goes beyond the range of one's own knowledge or observation is to take up an indefensible position. Wasn't it G. K. Chesterton, a man whose massive bulk made even the thought of mountain climbing unendurable, who said: "If a dozen honest men tell me that they have climbed the Matterhorn I am satisfied that the summit of that mountain is accessible, though I may never get there myself"? Long years ago there was a king of Siam who had a Dutch ambassador at his court. One day the ambassador, in describing his native country to the king, remarked that during the winter the water there became so hard that men could actually walk on it. The king at once flew into a rage. He was not prepared, he said, to credit so monstrous a falsehood; he had never seen such a thing happen; it was ridiculous, preposterous, impossible; the ambassador was surely out of his mind. Personal experience, you see, no matter of what sort, is apt to be limited, fragmentary, incomplete, and being so should never be made the basis of an absolute judgement.

Of religious experience that is certainly the case. When I look into my Bible, when I take up the hymn-book, when I read the story of the heroes of the Faith, I have to acknowledge that there are visions and vistas clearer and fairer than have ever come to me. Don't you have to do the same thing? J. B. Pratt sent to William James a questionnaire which asked, among other things, "Is God very real to you? . . . Do you feel that you have experienced His presence? . . . How vague or how distinct is it?" Then there followed the enquiry: "If you have had no such experience, do you accept the testimony of others who claim to have felt God's presence directly? Please answer this question with special care and in as great detail as possible." To which James replied: "Yes! The whole line of testimony on this point is so strong that I am unable to pooh-pooh it away."

And what of the place in the line where the testimony is extraordinarily clear and emphatic? What are we to make of Jesus

Christ? Is he deliberately deceiving us in what he tells us? Or was he himself deceived? Or is he a true and faithful witness? I see no way of evading that trilemma. It is absolutely inexorable. One way or another we must make our choice—deceived, deceiver, a true and faithful witness.

Am I speaking to any one who is without religious experience and for that reason disposed to be sceptical as to whether what is said in this pulpit and in others like it is not all a case of much cry and no wool? You tell me that you doubt whether there is anything in your life that deserves to be designated as religious experience. There are times in church when you feel like an alien and a stranger. You can sense that others round about you are stirred and moved but you are not. You can see by the spirit in which they sing, by the reverence with which they pray, by their response to each act of worship that the spiritual world is real and luminous to them, but it is neither real nor luminous to you. Well now, what about such people? Are you prepared to take the steps they have taken to acquire such experience? Do notice that I say "the steps they have taken." You don't just drift into religious experience. There are conditions to be observed before it can become yours. There is a sense—as the evangelicals will want to remind me—in which it is free as the air. Paul exultantly emphasized that when he said, "Not of works lest any man should boast; it is the gift of God." There is another sense in which it is only acquired and then developed and deepened by dint of surrender, dedication, discipline and devotion. Paul, in a passage of a different kind, emphasized that when he said, "Work out your own salvation with fear and trembling." Sensing something of the sort a member of my generation, the writer of many a scintillating and ironical poem with a barb in its concluding lines, May Richstone, has surprised her contemporaries by writing:

Back to the church of my fathers, I went—
The years away had been long—
Seeking an accrual of faith
To make my spirit strong.

I looked about me and I saw
Humble, devout folk there
Lifting transfigured faces up,
Drawing strength from prayer.

But no fund of faith was there for me,
Only emptiness and doubt;
For years I had put nothing in—
What could I hope to draw out!

When Alexander Whyte died his friend Norman Maclean wrote for *The Scotsman,* Edinburgh's leading newspaper, an appreciation of his character and work. I cut it out at the time for Whyte was one of my heroes. Here is an extract from it. "Walking along Princes Street"—is there a street quite like it in all the world?—"he was isolated in his own atmosphere—in the world, yet not of it. In the General Assembly he sat day by day— silent, wrapped in meditation, while the endless talk went on. He was there in the midst of it; but his soul dwelt apart. He had a gift of silence." That conveys some impression of the man Whyte was. Now mark this: A young minister, fresh from the Keswick Convention, a convention for the deepening of spiritual life, went into Whyte's study and spoke of his experiences with rapture, just as if the new Jerusalem had come. "Aye man," said Whyte, "it's a sair fecht to the last."

Does the road wind uphill all the way?
Yes, to the very end.

Dr. Inge, in writing of the Christian mystics, says that he cannot claim to have shared their wonderful experience of communion

with God, but he is honest enough and humble enough to acknowledge that if he had been a better man and had submitted himself
to a stricter spiritual regimen he might have done so.

In such a supremely important matter as this is we shall be well
advised to turn for light and leading to Jesus. He had a real and
vivid faith in God and he tells us what steps to take if we wish
to make such a faith our own. He emphasizes the conditions to be
observed, but what has surprised some, when it has been drawn
to their attention, is that on his showing the conditions are not so
much intellectual as they are moral. He nowhere promises the
vision of God to the clever and the sophisticated but to the pure
and simple of heart. With him the stress is not on mental struggle
but on moral earnestness and sincerity. "Blessed are the pure in
heart: for they shall see God." "I thank thee, O Father, for hiding
all this from the wise and learned and revealing it to the simple-
minded." Give good heed to that element in the teaching of Jesus.
Experience of God, he says, is the possession not of the sharp-witted
and the clear-headed but of the pure-hearted. As Unamuno
phrased it, "Goodness is the greatest single source of spiritual
clear-sightedness."

In this context there is another saying of Jesus of which too
much cannot be made. He was teaching in the temple at Jerusalem, was teaching with such originality and authority that his
hearers were at a loss to know what to think of him. They turned
to one another and asked, "How is it that this man has learning
when he has never studied?" How wide of the mark that query
was! They were seeking to explain Jesus in terms of physical
origins and mental processes. He bade them go deeper. They
thought they had to do with a pundit whereas he saw himself as
a moral agent. "My teaching," he said, "is not mine, but His who
sent me." And then he went on to add, "If any one has the will
to do God's will, he will find out whether my teaching is from God
or whether I speak on my own authority." See what he does! He

goes back of mental processes to volitional processes, back of the mind to the will. So many people think that first they must see and then they can serve, or that first they must know and then they can do. Jesus reverses the order. First we are to serve and then we shall see. First we are to do and then we shall know. It is not conviction first and action afterwards; it is the other way round; in action are the seeds and secret of conviction.

Or to put the point in another way, experiment and experience spring from the same root. "Doing and knowing are blood relations." Faith by its very character does not and cannot begin with certitude. It begins as an experiment and ends as an experience. Do you really want the authentic Christian experience? Then ask yourself whether you are prepared to make the Christian experiment. "If any one has the will to do God's will"—that is the first step on the path to religious conviction. It is possible to rely too much on what one can get out of books and arguments. There is a lesson to be learned from the case of the theologian who became so absorbed in arguing for the existence of God that he forgot to say his prayers. You may have been debating the religious issue off and on since you woke up to its existence in the years when you were in high school. How long is it since you went down on your knees and stayed on them for ten minutes? There is no question as to which is harder. And remember: Jesus does not promise religious certitude to the debater and speculator but to the person who puts his will as well as his mind into action. "Obedience is the organ of spiritual knowledge." Said a seeker after truth to Pascal, "I wish I had your creed, then I would live your life." And swift as a rapier thrust came the reply, "Live my life and you will soon have my creed." "Try it," cries Coleridge. "Do not talk to me of the evidences for Christianity. Try it." And didn't Chesterton once burst out, "Christianity has not been tried and found wanting; it has been found wanting and not tried"?

Take the case of Horace Bushnell—a young instructor at Yale,

beset by religious perplexities, unable to resolve his doubts, un-
settling the men in his classes, communicating to them his own
scepticism, and all the while reading about the religious issue
incessantly, discussing it whenever and wherever the opportunity
offered, but getting nowhere. And more and more as time passed
one question took shape in his mind: "What is the use of my
trying to get further knowledge, so long as I do not cheerfully
yield to what I already know?" It was a persistent question. He
could not fob it off. In the end it drove him to his knees to offer
the prayer: "O God, I believe there is an eternal difference between
right and wrong, and I hereby give myself up to do the right and
refrain from the wrong. I believe that Thou dost exist, and if
Thou canst hear my prayer and will reveal Thyself to me, I pledge
myself to do Thy will, and I make this pledge fully, freely and
forever." The rest of the story you probably know. One by one
his doubts were resolved and he became for his day and generation
a mighty prophet of the faith.

Perhaps there is something in that for you. Let action take the
place of speculation. You tell me that you do not know what to
believe about the Bible, about the divinity of Christ, about the
miracles, about prayer. Your religious perplexities are numerous
and genuine enough, I have no doubt; but what of your moral
certainties? In a world like this there are many things you do not
know and may never know, but there are some things you do
know. You know that love is better than hate, that loyalty is better
than treachery, that purity is better than impurity, that it is
always right to do the right and to abstain from the wrong. Are
you acting in accordance with those innate and immemorial convictions? And if not, are you prepared as God gives you grace and
strength to try to do so—to stand or fall by the noblest hypothesis,
"to follow right because of right in scorn of consequence"? In
particular, are you ready—and this is where I am out for a verdict—
to substitute the practice of religion for argument about it? If

you are, religious experience and conviction are bound in time to be yours. Christ has pledged his word that it will be so. "If any one has the will to do God's will, he will know." What David Livingstone said in another connection applies here. "It is the word of a gentleman of the most strict and sacred honor, and there's an end of it." Cries one of the New Testament writers, "No one who puts his trust in him will ever be disappointed; no one." That testimony comes to you black with the signatures of men and women during sixty generations.

> It were not hard, we think, to serve Him,
>   If we could only see!
> If He would stand with that gaze intense
>   Burning into our bodily sense,
> If we might look on that face most tender,
> The brow where the stars are turned to splendour;
> Might catch the light of His smile so sweet,
> And view the marks on His hands and feet,
>   How loyal we should be!
> It were not hard, we think, to serve Him,
>   If we could only see!
>
> It were not hard, He says, to see Him,
>   If we would only serve:
> "He that doeth the will of heaven,
> To him shall knowledge and sight be given."
> While for His presence we sit repining,
> Never we see His countenance shining:
> They who toil where His reapers be
> The glow of His smile may always see,
> And their faith can never swerve.
> It were not hard, He says, to see Him,
>   If we would only serve.

To that there seems to be nothing to add unless it is a sentence out of the last book in the Bible, "His servants shall serve Him: and they shall see His face."

Can We Believe in a Personal God?

FOR MANY the biggest problem in religion is how to believe in a personal God. Every thinking person is alive to it. Atheism has little attraction for the majority of us; it leaves unsolved more questions than it seems to solve. We believe that God, in some sense, exists, but we find it easier to conceive of a First Cause, a Principle of Order, some law or necessity or power at the centre of things, than to think of God in personal terms as One who actually addresses us, enters into intimate and reciprocal relationships with us, cares for and loves us like a father. Watching the crowds on Broadway, standing under a starry sky and pondering the vastness and variety of nature we wonder whether it can possibly be true that there is a God who speaks as I, who may be addressed as Thou, a God with personal attributes, with an insight, a concern, a plan for every individual, knowing him and his circumstances altogether.

There are reasons peculiar to our time which make faith of such a sort difficult. The whole modern tendency is in the direction of impersonal thinking and living. Consider the increasing depersonalization of industrial relationships since the beginning of the machine age; the desocialized life which millions live in great cities; the extent to which all our minds have been moulded and conditioned by the abstract methods and categories of science. It is not surprising that there is a disposition to view the world, as Bertrand Russell does, as a soulless machine which cares nothing for man's dreams and ideals but, blind to good and evil, rolls on its relentless way. The fact is that modern man has lost the sense of God as a Father and a Friend. To think of God in personal terms is, he feels, unscientific.

There is justification for the revolt of some against belief in a personal God. It is a revolt that not infrequently has praiseworthy motives. I am thinking of those who cannot and will not believe that which offends their reason and intelligence. Any description of God in crude sensory terms, the type of description college students submitted in reply to Dr. Leuba's questionnaires, they are obliged to reject. Here are two of the responses. "It may be a remnant of youth, but anyhow, every time I think of God there appears a vague image of a man, with all members of the body, just enormously large." "I think of God as having bodily form and being much larger than the average man. He has a radiant countenance beaming with love and compassion. He is erect and upright, fearless and brave." We all began with such images in our minds but unless we are intellectually dormant we have no alternative but to discard them. It is not only naïve but erroneous to think of God in physical, bodily terms.

This does not mean that we are debarred from thinking of Him as personal. To be sure, when we say that God is personal we mean that in certain respects He is like ourselves. Some will not hear of any such thing. They rule out any kind of anthropomorphism, that is, any tendency on man's part to think of God as like himself. But there are two kinds of anthropomorphism. The one is primitive and naïve—the early Greeks envisaging the gods on Olympus as eating, drinking, quarrelling, lusting, loving; the early Old Testament writers describing Jehovah as walking in the garden in the cool of the day, calling for Adam and Eve, shutting the door of the ark, wrestling with Jacob, bowing down His ear, making bare His arm, sitting in the heavens and laughing; Marc Connelly's play *Green Pastures* in which De Lawd has an office, and a chief assistant known affectionately as Gabe, and when De Lawd wants to know how things are going on the earth He has to go down and see.

That is one kind of anthropomorphism. It is artless and simple. It is man's attempt to conceive God and to do it in terms derived from his own experience. In what other terms can he do it? He has no words, no thoughts, no ideals, no symbols that are not human. The God of the savage is the kind of chief he would be himself if he had the opportunity. The God of the moralist is first and foremost a great Judge and Schoolmaster. The God of science is impersonal and inflexible Law. Such anthropomorphism is inevitable. It is impossible for man to think at all except in terms derived from his own experience.

But not all anthropomorphism is naïve and primitive. It takes maturer, finer, nobler forms. The early Greeks unhesitatingly ascribed to the gods their own petty meannesses and evil passions. Later, men like Socrates and Plato denounced this as blasphemy and attributed to God such qualities—human qualities they all are—as thought, purpose, consciousness, personality. Socrates and Plato would have been the first to acknowledge that they could not completely grasp the full significance of such terms in their application to God. They would readily have granted that man's thoughts, purposes, consciousness, personality are not as God's. Indeed they said again and again that it is God alone to whom these terms apply in their full and true significance.

Similarly with the prophets of Israel. Men like Amos and Hosea, Isaiah and Jeremiah took the highest and holiest qualities they knew and thought of God expressly and essentially in such terms.

The attributes of righteousness, justice, mercy, fatherly love they found in their own hearts. They recognized them as good and reverently accepted them as divine attributes. The noblest qualities in man, they said, are but reflections of the glory that is God. It may be objected that this is to make God in man's image, but consider: What better can we do than liken God to the very best we know or can conceive, always adding that our best hints at an excellence far beyond our reach? God's thoughts are not as our thoughts, nor His ways as our ways, but no higher category than our own rational and spiritual life is open to us in which to place Him. This is what we find not only in Greek thinkers and in Hebrew prophets but in Jesus. He everywhere assumes that God can be known and interpreted in terms of human thought and experience. He says, "If ye, being evil, know how to give good gifts to your children, how much more will your heavenly Father?" Mark what he does. He takes human fatherhood as a clue to the Fatherhood of God. He argues from the best in man to its infinity in God. He justifies us in concluding that the best in man is continuous with what is most fundamental in the Universe.

Because personal existence is the highest type of existence known to us, we think of God not as an impersonal force but as a living person, and mean when we say that God is personal that He knows and wills and loves and does all three perfectly. Our personalities are limited, are arbitrary, exclusive, individualistic, but these defects, which we are conscious of as defects, do not belong to personality as such. Personality is a matter of degree, a fact we recognize when we say of one man that "he is not much of a person" and of another that "he is a real person." With us personality is, or ought to be, in the making. We should be growing in knowledge and purpose and love. Yet however great the growth may be we all have to confess when we look into ourselves that we fall short in personal quality. God alone is the ideal

Personality, knowing, willing, loving to perfection, the One who realizes with a completeness which passes beyond our finite ability to comprehend, or even to imagine, all that we would wish to be ourselves. To say that God is personal is not to apply to Him an unworthy or limiting conception; it is to take what is finest and noblest in our consciousness and affirm its perfect existence in Him.

Right down the centuries this is what believing men and women have consistently done. One of the perennial convictions of religious faith is that the Universe is under the control of a loving purpose. Behind the harsh appearances of the world the believer finds a Friend. Wrote Gilbert Murray, the classical scholar, "As I see philosophy after philosophy falling into this unproven belief in the Friend behind phenomena, as I find that I myself cannot, except for a moment and by an effort, refrain from making the same assumption, it seems to me that perhaps we here too are under the spell of a very old ineradicable instinct." "I know," cries Job out of the depth of his trouble, "that my Redeemer liveth." The mother of Josiah Royce, crossing the continent in a covered wagon, was one day confronted with a terrible danger and yet somehow felt self-possessed and unafraid. "I had known what it was to believe in God," she wrote that night in her diary, "but now He came so near that I no longer simply believed in Him but knew His presence there. . . . That calm strength, that certainty of One near and all-sufficient hushed and cheered me."

I do not say that the testimony of religious experience to the personality of God has been unanimous. Much Eastern religion has been pantheistic, has identified God with nature and spurned as unworthy any suggestion that personal quality should be attributed to the Divine. Yet in the East as in the West the craving of the human heart is for a personal God. Sankara, the Indian philosopher, rejected the ascription of personality to God.

No human analogy, he maintained, can worthily represent God. But Sankara's mother, when she lay dying, told him that his impersonal Absolute meant nothing to her, that she could not think it, or see it, or get to it. What do you suppose Sankara did? He wrote for her a hymn to a personal deity to help her through the valley of the shadow. Indian religion is under the spell of a very old ineradicable instinct. Buddhism and Hinduism only became the religions of the people when they substituted for an impersonal Absolute a Being who could be adored as a Friend and worshipped as a Saviour. One of the greatest of Indians had this to say, "The Impersonal has no grip upon my heart", a cry matched by the declaration of D. W. Forrest: "The love of God ceases to have any meaning for the heart, if He ceases to be a Person for the mind."

Faith in a personal God is from first to last the faith of the Bible and the radiant centre of the Gospel. "Son of man, stand upon thy feet": the prophet felt himself addressed directly. "Save me, O God: for the waters are come in unto my soul": the Psalmist could make appeal to a sure and tried Friend. "My heart and my flesh cry out for the living God": there is the passionate hunger of an Old Testament saint. And when you cross from the Old Testament to the New what do you find? "When you pray, say, Our Father." It is as direct and as individual as that. "I know whom I have believed and I am persuaded that He is able to keep that which I have committed unto him against that day." It is as intimate and inward as that. "Lord, what wilt Thou have me do?" It is as pointed and as personal as that. There is One with whom we can enter into fellowship, to whom we can pray, by whom we are in mercy forgiven, on whom we can absolutely depend. Let us be very clear about this. Christian experience is possible only if God is personal and if we can maintain personal relationships with Him. The Christian lives by faith, prayer, love. His faith is only secondarily assent to a group of propositions; primarily it is trust in a Person who has drawn near to him supremely in Jesus Christ.

This faith comes to us for the most part not as a result of intellectual deduction or through argument and debate but in the thick of everyday experience. I knew a shepherd who told me that he came to realize the presence of God while walking over the hills and that he prayed himself through the troubles of his life. David Cairns tells how such faith was awakened in him. He was coming back from a seaside holiday with his father and mother. He had a fishing line which had got into a desperate tangle and he was doing his futile best to disentangle it in the railway carriage when his father, who had been watching him, said, "Let me try it, David." He handed it over, and like magic the line spread out in his father's hands and he got it back about as good as ever in two or three minutes. This is the son's comment made years afterwards. "Neither of us, I daresay, had any idea that we were giving or getting a picture that would be with me at least all my days to show how God deals with us His children and how we should deal with Him."

Others again, like the mother of Josiah Royce, testify that faith came to them in critical moments when their need was great, and that it was then they discovered that behind phenomena there is a Friend, a Helper of men and women, nearest at hand when the worst has to be encountered. Years ago now Newton Clarke offered the judgement that it is not through the vastness of the universe that we learn to trust in a personal God; it is in the life of the soul that we begin to believe in the will of God, the wisdom of God and the love of God; it is there that our personality finds rest in His.

It is a mistake to associate faith in a personal God solely with questions of theology. It is a mistake to make it only a matter of reading and philosophizing, of discussion and debate. Look for faith in a personal God as a gift out of the ordinary experience of everyday life, as the mother of Josiah Royce did, as my shepherd friend did, as David Cairns did, as multitudes have done. And if you are confused in mind, or bewildered by doubt, or if you have fallen into sin, and still long to find God, do something very simple, so simple that we all forget its efficacy. Get down on your knees, wait till all the voices in your heart are still, and then say, "Our Father, who art in heaven . . . " Get down on your knees not once or twice but often. That is the old way, the best way, the sure way to belief in the presence and power of the God and Father of our Lord Jesus Christ.

What Is the Case for Personal Survival?

ASTER SUNDAY finds the churches filled to overflowing. The cynic thinks he has the explanation. The Easter Festival is a fashion parade. It is notorious that it brings people to church who will not be seen again in twelve months. It is like a national holiday, celebrated in conformity with long established custom, stirring up agreeable associations in the mind, but otherwise making hardly any impression of a profound or lasting sort.

So the cynic argues. There is truth in what he says but it is not the whole truth. Other factors and motives are at work. It is a sound instinct that brings us here to-day. The Easter music and the Easter message strike a responsive chord; they meet a deep, even if inarticulate, craving of the human spirit. There is something in us which needs to hear them and which is the better for hearing them. There is a faith at the heart of them which acts on us like a tonic, which lifts these lives of ours to new levels of dignity and meaning, and inspires all who share it with courage and hope.

Not that all share the Easter faith. There are some who say that they have no belief in or wish for a life after death. They have no objection to being extinguished but would prefer it. They have no wish for any further experience on the other side of the grave. They feel that they will have had enough of the business of living when the time comes for them to die. H. G. Wells frequently remarked that he could never understand why so many people seemed to find the prospect of a final, personal death unendurable. It impressed him as egoism. He had, he said, no such appetite for a separate immortality.

The only immortality Wells believed in was the immortality a man achieves through his influence on others. It is a belief that has a strong appeal—survival in our children and in our children's children; living on in minds made better by our presence; contributing to the progress of humanity through the causes we serve, the institutions we help to build, the forces for good we set in motion. "Why do you commiserate with me?" asked an English mother when friends sympathized with her over the son she had lost in the Battle for Britain. "He lived for twenty happy, clean years and then he died for England. What better could he have done than that?" There is a strong appeal in such a sentiment; but see what it in fact signifies. It involves an endless succession of gallant souls of whom none is used as an end in himself but only as an instrument. Each serves the purposes of the future—a future which is always remote. What we want to know is what happened to that boy? To be sure, he will live on in the proud memory of his mother and friends, but is he himself still existent somewhere? Is he the self-conscious, individualized, creative personality he once was?

Men may have no appetite for a separate immortality for themselves but when death invades their home, snatches away one who was at the centre of their world and indispensable to it, they are loath to believe that it is "good-bye for ever." H. G. Wells judged that the hope of personal survival was due to egoism. Why, he

asked, should we presume to expect that our personalities will
persist? What he overlooked was that it is not when we are selfish
but when love has taken full possession of our hearts that the desire for immortality awakes. Love cannot brook separation or
endure to think of extinction. In our hearts there is an unappeas-
able yearning to be reunited with those to whom we owe what is
best and happiest in our lives.

Tolstoy was giving expression to this universal hunger when
in *War and Peace* he had Pierre say to Prince Andrey, "I feel
that I cannot disappear . . . that indeed I shall always be." And
Andrey replies: "Yes, that's Herder's theory, but it's not that
convinces me; life and death are what have convinced me. What
convinces me is seeing a creature dear to me, and bound up with
me . . . and all at once that creature suffers, is in agony, and ceases
to be. . . . What for? It cannot be that there is no answer! One is
convinced of the necessity of a future life, not by argument but
when one goes hand-in-hand with some one, and all at once that
some one slips away yonder into nowhere, and you are left facing
into the abyss and looking down into it. And I have looked down
into it." What, one wonders, would H. G. Wells have made of
that? Love, not egoism, is the mainspring of the desire for life
beyond death.

> What is excellent,
> As God lives, is permanent;
> Hearts are dust, hearts' loves remain;
> Heart's love will meet again.

No coercive proof can be advanced in support of such a faith.
It cannot be demonstrated scientifically any more than it can be
disproved scientifically. But feeling is older in human nature than
intellect, and as Pascal pointed out, "The heart has its own reasons
which the reason does not know." Its yearnings, its insights, its

intuitions are not contrary to reason but deeper, than reason. The final assurance of personal survival springs not from the demand of the intellect nor from the prompting of the conscience, but from the hunger of the heart. Said James Martineau, "We do not believe in immortality because we have proved it, but, we forever try to prove it because we believe in it."

And with the hunger of the heart there goes the testimony of the reason. Why, in generation after generation, have poets, philosophers, prophets affirmed their belief in immortality? Because it seemed to them that the very rationality of the world required it. Because they were unable to convince themselves by any kind of theory or logic that man's ultimate destiny is a rendezvous with the dust. Because, knowing the brightness with which man's spirit can burn in his mortal body, they refused to concede that at death it could be extinguished, like a candle gutted by a passing wind. Reason insists that our life here is but the prelude to a richer, completer life hereafter. Otherwise there is a hollowness at the core of things, a want of consistency, and Shakespeare's dirge is justified:

> Golden lads and girls all must
> As chimney sweepers, come to dust.

The ground plan of the universe is unreasonable if we are called into being, permitted to start our development as human spirits, given glimpses of greater possibilities, only to have our growth ruthlessly terminated by death, to be cut off, as William James put it, when we are "just getting fit to live." The mind cannot make sense of such a hypothesis or rest in it.

Listen to Socrates! "Let a man be of good cheer about his soul, if only it be arrayed in its proper jewels—in temperance and justice, nobility and truth. Thus adorned it will be ready, when

the hour comes, to start on its journey to the other world. And
there it will dwell in mansions far fairer than here; it will be
like going from captivity to home." Listen to Tennyson!

> Thou wilt not leave us in the dust,
> Thou madest man, he knows not why.
> He thinks he was not made to die.
> And Thou hast made him: Thou art just.

Doesn't your mind make the same kind of affirmation? Think of a
Beethoven triumphing over deafness and enriching the whole
world with divine melody. Think of a Wilfred Grenfell devoting
his life to sacrificial service in Labrador. Think of Wendell
Willkie and the dream of one world that lured him—of Wendell
Willkie dead at fifty-two. Think of the finest and best persons
you have known. What has become of them? Do they survive
only in their influence? All those patiently developed talents and
gifts—have they been wiped out? Was the spirit that was in them
utterly extinguished at death? Beethoven's music living on but
not Beethoven. The work Grenfell established surviving but not
Grenfell. What could be less rational? Dowered with such gifts,
made to live such wonderful lives, and then rotting in the grave!
And what about Jesus? Was a personality like his swept at death
into nothingness? Thirty-three years and all was over. Believe
that and is there anything at the heart of things save frustration
and unreason, a riddle for which there is no explanation? But who
can believe that? The mind revolts at the thought. "What shall
we say of the Power behind the universe," cried Canon Streeter,
"if it treats the individuality of heroic souls like oyster-shells at a
banquet, whisked from the table to make room for the next
course?"

With the hunger of the heart and the testimony of the reason
there goes the witness of religion. It is a double witness involving a

WHAT IS THE CASE FOR PERSONAL SURVIVAL?

belief about the nature of man and a belief about the character of God. Take the religion with which we are most familiar, the Christian religion. One of its foundational principles is the value of every individual in the sight of God. It stresses the worth, the incalculable worth of human personality. "What," asks Jesus, "shall it profit a man"—not a rich man, not a wise man, not a good man, but a man—"if he shall gain the whole world and lose his own soul?" "There is joy in the presence of the angels of God over one sinner"—one fallen man—"that repenteth." If man has such intrinsic value it is inconceivable that death should be the end of him. As a great hymn has it:

> Not spilt like water on the ground,
> Not wrapped in dreamless sleep profound,
> Not wandering in unknown despair
> Beyond Thy voice, Thy arm, Thy care,
> Not left to die like fallen tree:
> Not dead, but living unto Thee.

That is the joyous, confident hope we find everywhere in the New Testament. On the other hand, if man is only an animal of a superior breed, hopes like these are the merest imaginings and the history of religion, and of the Christian religion in particular, is just a chapter in mythology.

It is the true conception of human nature that is at stake here. I have said that H. G. Wells had no use for the doctrine of personal immortality. In one of his books he poked fun at it. "When Mrs. Bloggs sits in her back pew and hears the blessed hope of immortality coming from the pulpit, it is Mrs. Bloggs herself, body and soul, thirty-five, a little faded, kindly and tending to put on weight, who is to live, she understands, eternal in the heavens. Dressed rather differently perhaps, more in the bridesmaid style, but otherwise the same." What is significant in that bit of writing is not Mrs. Bloggs' misconceptions of immortality; it is H. G.

Wells' misconception of Mrs. Bloggs—his evident opinion that in so homely a body it would be absurd to suppose there could be personal possibilities of more than local and ephemeral importance. But that is the whole point of the Christian witness. It sees in human personality, no matter how commonplace or limited, august possibilities. For Wells the frog crushed by a cart-wheel, the fly drowning in the cream jug, and Mrs. Bloggs sitting in her back pew are all alike incidental experiments to be swept aside and forgotten. Wells forgot that what we do for man and what we do with man depends ultimately on what we think of man, of his nature, whence he comes and whither he is going. Without immortality human life is liable to lose its significance and sanctity, and men are apt to be used as "hands," tools, cannon fodder.

The witness of religion involves a belief about the character of God as well as the nature of man. A human father will not consent to the loss of any of his children. Are we to suppose that God will? "Would it not be blasphemy," wrote Wordsworth in his bereavement, "to say we have more of love in our nature than He has?" "Can it be," Dr. Fosdick once asked from this pulpit, "that God is the most unscrupulous waster in the universe—making great personalities only to throw them utterly away?" Readers of Olive Schreiner's *Story of an African Farm* will recall how Bonaparte came on Waldo when he was engrossed over a little mechanical device, an affair of wheels and chips of wood, which it had taken the lad nine months to put together, and how after making a show of interest in it Bonaparte tramped on the machine and crushed it in the sand. Is that how God treats those whom He has made? Will He do what we loathe and despise a Bonaparte for doing? A parent would never consent to the extinction of a child. Is God likely to think of such a thing?

It is a powerful argument. The only way to attack it is by denying the premise on which it rests. If God and man can enter into fellowship, man must matter to God. And if he matters to God he must share God's eternity. This is the conviction we find in Jesus. "If ye then, being evil, know how to give good gifts to your children, how much more your heavenly Father." He stakes his confidence in the life beyond death on the character of God, His goodness, His faithfulness, His fatherliness. "Thou wilt not leave us in the dust"—that is the affirmation of faith in the fatherliness of God.

And so we come to the central feature of the Easter message—the Resurrection of Jesus. The conviction of the heart, the testimony of the reason, the witness of religion all weigh with us, but what weighs with us most is the joyous fact we commemorate this morning. The noblest life of which we have any record did not come to a full stop at Calvary. The crucifixion was not the last word in that matchless story. God raised up Jesus from the dead, and by his resurrection vindicated the cause of righteousness, endorsed everything for which Jesus stood, demonstrated that the universe is on the side of goodness and truth. God raised up Jesus from the dead, and by his resurrection took the terror from the grave, broke the power of sorrow and tragedy, inspired the assurance that life is not doomed to end in frustration and futility, that death does not write Finis over everything, that, on the contrary, it is the door which opens on wonder upon wonder—on life and love and God. God raised up Jesus from the dead, and by his resurrection gave to the world not a dead teacher but a living Lord. In John Masefield's play, The *Trial of Jesus*, the Roman centurion who stood at the foot of the Cross talks with Pilate's wife just after the crucifixion. "Do you think he is dead?" she asks him. "No, lady," he answers, "I don't." "Then where is he?" And the reply she receives is, "Let loose in the world, lady, where neither Roman nor Jew can stop his truth." That is not fiction, that is fact. For sixty generations that has been the Christian persuasion.

Jesus lives and reigns. His presence and power are still available. His promise still stands, "Lo, I am with you always." What an assurance is this! "Hallelujah! for the Lord God omnipotent reigneth!"

Why Does God Hide Himself?

"VERILY Thou art a God that hidest Thyself," exclaimed Isaiah. How often through the centuries that cry has risen to human lips! Of late we ourselves have not been unfamiliar with it. Cast your mind back of Pearl Harbor to the early summer of 1940. Those were days when we looked abroad on a crazy and disordered world in which little nations were going down like ninepins before ruthless and conscienceless aggression, men were lying wounded and dying on far-flung battlefields, women and children were being driven from their homes and bombed and machine-gunned as they fled for safety. And God did not intervene. The awful silence of heaven remained unbroken. We pleaded with Him to manifest Himself and defend the right; as the crisis deepened, special days were set aside for intercessory prayer and the churches were crowded with men and women addressing earnest entreaties to the Most High. Yet the aggressor marched on, apparently undeterred, from one conquest to another. What wonder that some like H. G. Wells complained bitterly. "He is an ever-absent help in time of trouble," while others found themselves declaring in their perplexity, "Verily Thou art a God that hidest Thyself."

Nor with the coming of peace, an uneasy and insecure kind of peace, has the cry lost relevance, as the following sentences from a recent book will demonstrate. "What interests me is not whether God exists, but, assuming He exists, what He is like, and what on earth He is up to at the present moment. I mean 'what on earth' quite literally. Of the home life of God I know nothing, and I am equally ignorant of His relations with other planets and universes. But I am concerned with this world in which I happen to live, and I consider it important to have as clear a picture as possible of the person who made it." Whatever you may think of that, there is a man for whom God is perplexingly unobtrusive and reticent, and there are great numbers of people like him.

It is the chaotic condition of the world that gives rise to such confusion and bewilderment. For that reason, we do well to recognize that from the beginning of things God has been wont to conceal Himself. *Consider how He hides Himself in nature.* In saying that I do not forget that for many nature is the very handwriting of God. Wordsworth felt among the great mountains the power of an unseen and eternal Presence, and centuries ago a Psalmist in Israel sang, "The heavens declare the glory of God and the firmament showeth His handiwork." It would be absurd to deny that to some persons God discloses Himself in the splendour and loveliness of the world. To some, but not to all. What of those for whom nature is not a transparent screen but an obscuring medium—red in tooth and claw, cruel, relentless, indifferent to moral issues? The laws of nature are the same for the good man as for the bad; the floods drown both; the lightning does not go out of the way of either. With this in mind there are those who deny that there is any revelation of God in nature. We may not be prepared to go as far, but perhaps we would agree that it is only when we see with the eyes of Christ that the message of nature can be clearly deciphered.

Dr. H. H. Farmer has pointed out that there is a certain effort of mind necessary to become aware of God in the world around us.

He instances the streams of men and women who pass along the roads on any bright Sunday morning to enjoy the refreshments and delights of the countryside. "If it is true that the beauty of tree and flower, of birdsong and sunshine, is the free bounty of God, it is strange that these people should be entirely unaware of it, as indeed most of them are. If only God would, so to say, sign some of His gifts. If only, like the artist, He would put His signature at the foot of some masterpiece of colouring in the sky, or like the musician, have His name appropriately announced prior to every song of the lark! But He does not. Verily He is a God that hideth Himself!"

Consider, too, how God hides Himself in history. Cromwell said to the man whom he appointed to tutor his son, "I would have him taught a little history." We know why he said what he did. He believed that the study of history inclined one to a sane, balanced and reverent judgement. But not all the lessons that history teaches are lessons that inspire and quicken faith. So often when we delve into the story of the past, what do we find? —might triumphing over right, the race to the swift and the battle to the strong, truth on the scaffold and wrong on the throne, Christ on a Cross and Caesar in a palace. Indeed, in regard to the interpretation of history, two schools of thought compete for our support. One contends that the world is built on moral foundations, that in the long run it is well with the good and ill with the wicked, that for cruelty, injustice and oppression a price has to be paid at the last. The other protests that the voice which comes to us across the centuries is not the paean of triumphant right and justice, but a doleful song, an ancient tale of wrong; that the one penalty which we can with certainty pronounce against the unjust man or nation lies in the fact of injustice, that to be corrupt and oppressive is its own punishment; that the only fixed law of retribution is that of the terribly emphatic and final sentence, "He that is unjust let him be unjust still, and he that is filthy let him be filthy still."

Now the fact that men should differ over such an issue is in itself abundant proof that God moves in a mysterious way in history. There is a notable passage in Newman's *Apologia* where he acknowledges that he has extreme difficulty in finding God in the march of contemporary events. He has no doubt of the universal reality of God, none at all, but as soon as he seeks for Him in the outside world he feels puzzled and appalled. "If I looked into a mirror, and did not see my face, I should have the sort of feeling which actually comes upon me, when I look into this living, busy world and see no reflection of its Creator."

Consider, also, how even in grace God hides Himself. Luther has a favourite phrase which keeps cropping up in his *Letters* and *Table Talk*. He repeatedly refers to God as the "hidden God," the idea in his mind being that God is essentially unknowable unless and until He takes the initiative and in loving, condescending grace reveals Himself to sinful man. And this Luther believed God had done. In Christ the hidden God had made Himself known. That is our belief too, but where have we to look for this divine revelation? To the manger of an inn, to the guise of a peasant, to a man broken on a cross. It must have been hard to discern the Son of God in a Galilean carpenter. And just because he appeared incognito some failed to recognize him, though it was by him chiefly that the awful silence of heaven was broken. Indeed, if some failed to recognize him, others were sorely mystified by him. Are you the Messiah? they kept asking him. Let us know for certain. Give us some infallible sign. Put a stop to our hesitation and indecision. If you are the Christ, tell us plainly.

In nature, in history, in grace God hides Himself. Why? That question is bound to arise. And there are considerations to take into account which are not unhelpful. This for instance: What kind of God would he be whom we could completely comprehend, whose movements in nature and history were all known to us, and whose Being provoked no suggestion either of shuddering awe or of impenetrable mystery? That is the only God some people have. They talk of Him and to Him as if He were a man on the street. They allow themselves unlimited licence of dogmatic affirmation concerning the most profound matters. You can never catch them out. They have a solution, generally a slick one, for every problem that raises its head. But their God is not the God of the Bible. The God of the Bible is never obvious. His ways are not as our ways; His thoughts are not as our thoughts; His judgements are an abyss; clouds and thick darkness are about Him; and it is not by searching that we find Him out.

It must be so. It must always be so. We can be plain, precise, specific while we are dealing with what is finite, but as soon as we begin to touch the fringe of the infinite there is:

> A deep beyond the deep,
> And a height beyond the height,
> And our hearing is not hearing,
> And our seeing is not sight.

"Gentlemen," James Denney would say to his students, some of whom fondly imagined their divinity studies would all be over in the space of three years, "Gentlemen, to study infinity requires eternity." Centuries before Denney, Plato, a persistent and passionate seeker after God, declared, "The Father and Maker of this whole it is hard to find, and when one has found Him to declare Him to all is impossible."

Some of us are afraid of the word "agnosticism," perhaps because we fail to appreciate that there is a true as well as a false agnosticism. There is a reverent agnosticism which is the very soul of religion, and which consists in humble recognition of the fact that the resources of human thought and language, even at their highest and best, are woefully inadequate to express all the truth and meaning concerning God and His ways with men. Such *Christian* agnosticism finds classical expression in the wondering cry of Paul, "O the depth of the riches both of the wisdom and knowledge of God! how unsearchable are His judgements, and His ways past finding out!"

Then, again, the fact that God hides Himself is surely part of the probation of life. Some time ago I came across a remarkable piece of writing. It is from the pen of a priest of the Russian Orthodox Church. "The other day I heard some one say that a meteor had fallen somewhere in the wilderness of Siberia and blasted up by the roots miles upon miles of big timber. In Siberia, in the wilderness, where no one was made to feel His power and His will! Why didn't it fall somewhere else, say—on the Kremlin? Why does He not emerge and assert Himself as He did in the days of old? Don't you suppose if He made Himself known, people would flock back to Him? Of course they would. Yet here we are, His servants, waiting, waiting, and nothing happens. The heavens are silent; the earth is silent, the stars are silent, everything is silent."

That is tragic as well as dramatic. Of what does it remind you? I know of what it reminds me. "Command that these stones be made bread. Cast yourself down from the pinnacle of the temple. Be the sort of king they want you to be. Mount a charger and ride into Jerusalem as its Emancipator and Prince. If you are the Christ—out with it, tell them plainly." But no, he would not be the sort of king they wanted him to be. He withdrew himself from them when they clamoured for him to show his hand. And those withdrawals are the testing points of life. They reveal of what metal we are made. They uncover the character of our motives, the quality of our aims, the range and extent of our staying power. We do well to recall that Jesus himself had experience of these withdrawals. Who among us can interpret, not to say exhaust, the significance of the cry, "My God, my God, why hast Thou forsaken me?"

Besides, if God were never to hide Himself, if the element of mystery were completely eliminated from life, if we knew with mathematical certainty and precision that God exists, that right will eventually triumph over wrong, that there is another and better world beyond this, what place would be left for the exercise of the thing we call faith? I think of Donald Hankey writing from a trench in Flanders in 1914, "Faith is betting your life that there is a God," and of the case he goes on to state: The odds are all against you, the shells screaming over your head seem to mock at you, and there are comrades by your side who smile at you for a simpleton, but you hold on. You refuse either to give in or to give up, for you know that to surrender faith is to make the final surrender. It means subscription to the judgement that there is no sense and no purpose in life or history, that the whole tangled story of the race is a "tale told by an idiot, full of sound and fury, signifying nothing."

Take account of one more consideration. The darkness may not be above or around us but within us. It is impossible to be intellectually certain if we are morally unclean. How, in the case of his own people and times, did Isaiah explain these divine withdrawals? He had an explanation ready to hand. "Your sins," he made bold to tell them, "have separated between you and your God, and your iniquities have hid His face from you." The principle is timeless and in its application universal. Evil carries with it its own tremendous disqualifications. Of all spiritual things it is true that "now we see through a glass darkly," but the sinful character of our life increases the obscurity. The carnal mind, says Paul, is at enmity against God; it cannot know God;

by its very nature it is precluded from such knowledge. H. R. Mackintosh put the same law of the spiritual life into twentieth century terms when he wrote: "Is it not a familiar fact that our assurance of immortality wavers and flickers in secret concord with our habits? Does not our sense of God wax and wane with our loyalty to duty and our practice of private prayer?"

There is no call to worship more challenging than that of the question and answer to be found in the twenty-fourth Psalm. "Who shall ascend into the hill of the Lord? or who shall stand in His holy place? He that hath clean hands, and a pure heart; who hath not lifted up his soul unto vanity, nor sworn deceitfully. He shall receive the blessing from the Lord, and righteousness from the God of his salvation."

It is the same affirmation that our Lord makes, though in more positive fashion. "Blessed are the pure in heart: for they shall see God." Goodness, according to Jesus, is the primary source of spiritual clear-sightedness. The beatific vision is granted neither to the sharp-witted nor to the clear-headed but to the simple-hearted. "I thank Thee, O Father, . . . because Thou hast hid these things from the wise and prudent, and hast revealed them unto babes. Even so, Father: for so it seemed good in Thy sight."

Christ's supreme gift to men is the gift of a cleansed heart. He breaks the power of sin and frees us from its weight and impediment. And with growth in grace there is ever-increasing growth in vision. The pure in heart, though they see God here and now, shall see Him hereafter as they have never seen Him yet. "Now we see through a glass darkly, but then face to face." When redemption has wrought its perfect work, and their moral nature attains unto the fullness of the measure of the stature of their Lord, "His servants shall serve Him: and they shall see His face."

Does God Guide Us?

Once in London I saw two Cockneys stop in front of a church, their attention arrested by an announcement on its bulletin board. It was the title of the next Sunday's sermon and it read "Is There a God?" I overheard one of them remark to his neighbour as he pointed to the preacher's name on the bulletin board, "Is there a God? Blimey, wouldn't it be a caution if he said there ain't?"

To-day I raise the question, "Does God Guide Us?" Nobody, I am certain, expects me to come forward with a negative reply. I believe God does guide us. I have put the sermon title in the form of a question because it is a real question for lots of people. It is not a simple matter to believe that there is a pattern to our living which God is weaving, that He has a design fo_ the world at large and for us as individuals, that there is a particular as well as a general providence so that a man may know God's will both in his character *and* in his career. John Oxenham wrote:

> Not for one single day
> Can I discern my way,
>   But this I surely know,—
> Who gives the day,
> Will show the way,
>   So I securely go.

It is comforting to think about but hard to credit

We all know why. Science has shown the universe to be so vast that it has dwarfed man, has reduced his stature and made him seem by comparison insignificant and unimportant. "A microscopic dot in the vast expanse of space," is how one scientist describes the earth, and he goes on to relate how on this microscopic dot infinitesimal particles of impure carbon and water stir slightly for an instant of cosmic time, and then are dissolved back into the elements from which they were originally and fortuitously compounded. We are those infinitesimal particles.

We ought not to allow ourselves to be intimidated by this materialistic reading of the human situation. It plays into the hands of the totalitarian philosophers and is death to the whole democratic concept of the individual and of the worth of the individual. Size is no criterion of value. Bulk is no indication of worth. Man may be a reed but, as Pascal said, he is a thinking reed. Mind has achieved extraordinary triumphs over matter. Why should not the Cosmic Mind be a master of detail? If the telescope is a revelation of the immensity of the universe the microscope is a reminder of the care devoted to the minutest detail. To suppose that the powers of God are inadequate to His responsibilities is to think of Him in terms that are too human. It is to make God in our image. It is to assume that He is limited as we are limited in interest and knowledge. If God is great to the point of absolute infinity there can be no creature in all His mighty universe of whom He is not perpetually cognizant and conscious.

This is the faith we encounter everywhere in the Bible. Human affairs, it says, are under Divine direction. The universe is a moral universe in which God is working out His righteous purposes. The nations are not at the mercy of chance; nor are they in the grip of an impersonal force; they are under the guiding hand of

God. For the Hebrew prophets history is not an affair of cycles. They see God as in it and over it and using it for redemptive ends. It was into this heritage of faith that Jesus entered. Of his belief in the Divine Providence there can be no doubt. It is God, he teaches, who makes the sun rise and the rain fall. He clothes the lilies, provides for the birds, numbers the hairs of our heads. He knows our needs, and as His children we ought to pray to Him about them. We ought to say, "Lead us not into temptation" and "Give us this day our daily bread." But as soon as we pray in such terms we are committed to belief in a personal providential relation between God and man. We see the world not as an iceberg but as a ship, not as drifting but as being steered, not as the plaything of Crass Casualty but as guided by a conscious Mind.

Nor is this purely Biblical teaching. The Stoics held that the world is a unity of order and providence, not a welter of alternate combination and dispersion. In one of the *Dialogues* Plato says: "Let us begin, then, by asking whether all this which men call the Universe is left to the guidance of an irrational and random chance, or, on the contrary, as our fathers declared, is ordered and governed by a marvellous Intelligence and Wisdom." What follows leaves no room for doubt as to Plato's conviction. Belief in Providence has been a characteristic of most religions and of many philosophies, ancient and modern. Moreover, even when people surrender faith in a personal God they still incline to hold on to the idea of some all-controlling, over-ruling power shaping human destiny. The revived interest in astrology, a notable and depressing feature of our time, is evidence of the tenacity with which the mind clings to the idea that every circumstance and situation in life is under a higher than human control. Explicit teaching that everything is the result of blind mechanism or sheer chance has never really grasped and held the minds of men for long; such teaching is usually the outcome of pure theory, or of a despair which marks the beginning at least of a failure in the life impulse itself.

In the Bible it is not just a general providence but a particular providence that is taught. We read of God speaking directly to individuals, ordering their steps, assigning them tasks, disclosing to them His purpose and will. Thus Joseph's brethren sold him into Egypt. It was a mean act but he saw the hand of God in it, for years afterwards, when he made himself known to his brethren and they were abashed in his presence, he told them: "It was not you that sent me hither, but God." Thus, in his second missionary journey, Paul was specially conscious of unseen leadership. He went through Phrygia and Galatia without preaching, having been "prevented by the Holy Spirit." He planned to go into Bithynia but "was stopped again by the Spirit." Wondering where God was leading him he turned west and came to the sea at Troas. There he had a dream which he took for the guiding hand of God and he sailed at once for Europe. He could not have known, no man then alive could have known, that the centre of the world's life was soon to move west and north and that Europe, not Asia, was about to become the commercial and colonizing centre of the world. From the point of view of the Christian Mission it was a strategic move of the utmost importance but it was not made on Paul's own initiative. He was guided in those directions and to those areas where his work was to have the most enduring consequences.

From generation to generation men and women have affirmed their faith in a particular providence. Their testimony is that they have been guided in the big decisions of life. "I came about," wrote Robert Louis Stevenson, referring to a turning-point in his soul's career, "like a well-handled ship. There stood at the wheel that unknown Steersman whom we call God." This sense of a Divine purpose enfolding the life has sometimes been associated with little things—the writing of a letter, the paying of a visit, a chance remark. The experience of Dr. Albert Schweitzer is a case in point. He was trying to settle on his life-work. One night, he came across on his desk in college a green-covered magazine of the Paris Missionary Society and, in the act of putting it aside to get on with his studies, he opened it mechanically and caught sight of an article headed, "The Needs of the Congo Mission." "It was"—the account is Schweitzer's own—"by Alfred Boegner, the President of the Paris Missionary Society, an Alsatian, and contained a complaint that the Mission had not enough workers to carry on the work in the Gabon, the northern province of the Congo Colony. The writer expressed his hope that the appeal would bring some of those 'on whom the Master's eyes already rested' to a decision to offer themselves for this urgent task. The conclusion ran: 'Men and women who can reply simply to the Master's call, "Lord, I am coming," these are the people whom the Church needs!' " Says Schweitzer, "My search was over." So, all the splendid service at Lambaréné turned on a green-covered magazine. Schweitzer had no doubt that he was divinely led to it and through it to his life-work.

Sometimes the guidance is obvious and unmistakable, but not always. The Hand of God may be at the tiller of our life, steering us this way or that, and we may be unaware of the fact. In instance after instance it is seen not in outward, dramatic interventions but in the quiet succession of apparently natural events. Men commonly associate the Divine Providence with unexpected impulses and sudden promptings, with instructions to go somewhere or do something. What we are apt to forget is that God speaks to us most and influences us most in everyday situations, and particularly through challenging experiences which awaken us to the value and meaning of life or which call for dedication to a worthy cause or involve us in a specific piece of service.

Horace Bushnell preached a famous sermon entitled *Every Man's Life a Plan of God*. He based it on the sentence which Isaiah represents God as addressing to Cyrus the Persian: "I girded thee, though thou has not known me." God guides many a man, as He guided Cyrus, God uses many a man for great ends, as He used Cyrus, though the man, like Cyrus, does not know it.

Frequently it happens that the guidance is sensed only in retrospect. Many of us, looking back, reading the book of our lives chapter by chapter, can see how our path has been directed. There are happenings we can interpret in no other way. Some may call them coincidence but we are sure that a higher influence was at work. F. W. Robertson, Prince of preachers, wanted to be a soldier, as his father and grandfather had been, and as his three brothers were. But he could not secure a commission and finally took his father's advice and the advice of a friend and went up to Oxford to prepare for the Christian ministry. Five days after his arrival in Oxford the commission came. He longed to accept it but felt he had pledged himself to be a minister and could not go back on his pledge. Nobody now doubts that the ministry was his true calling or that if ever a man was designed for it Robertson was. That he himself came to feel this is apparent from a document found among his papers after his death which reads: "If I had not met a certain person, I should not have changed my profession; if I had not known a certain lady, I should not probably have met this person; if that lady had not had a delicate daughter who was disturbed by the barking of my dog, if my dog had not barked that night, I should now have been in the dragoons or fertilizing the soil of India. Who can say that these things were not ordered?"

All this prompts the question: If there is a particular as well as a general providence and God has purposes for our lives, how may we know them? We shall know them if we are in touch with God, if the lines of communication between us and Him are open, if we are at pains to learn and do His Will. God has sometimes spoken clearly to men who have been careless and prayerless but for the most part daily guidance only comes to those who daily seek it. The Quakers, who believe so strongly in the Inner Light, say in their *Book of Discipline:* "Our power to perceive the light of God is, of all our powers, the one which we need most to cultivate and develop. As exercise strengthens the body and education enlarges the mind, so the spiritual faculty within us grows as we use it in seeing and doing God's Will." It is when we are absorbed in the here and now that we become insensitive to the voices of God and sceptical about the unseen leadership. On the other hand, when prayer is real and we are spiritually alert we pass from one task to another quietly and without haste, sustained by the sense of God's presence and sure of His hand on our life. It is this that explains the serenity of Jesus. He lived so close to God that he knew at every turn what God wanted him to do next and could speak simply and naturally about his Father's business. He went from day to day and from duty to duty in complete self-command because he was never without the consciousness of Divine resource and sought and cultivated it constantly.

Seeking guidance from God does not mean, however, that we are exempted from using our own best judgement. As the writer of *Green Pastures* puts it, "I guess de Lord means us to figure out a few things for ourselves." Divine inspiration is given to enlighten rather than supersede our powers of rational and moral judgement. If we have to make a big decision ours is the responsibility for getting to know the facts of the case and thinking the thing through. Impulses and hunches should not be accepted blindly as direct voices of God. They ought first to be examined and approved by the conscience and the reason. Any decision we reach based on intelligence is a decision we have been helped to arrive at by God. Why did we get our intelligence if not for use? A comment made by Dr. Farmer will bear repetition. "We have not infrequently heard the prayer in pietistic circles, at the opening of business, 'May we have no ideas of our own,'—a prayer which, as a friend once tartly remarked, is only too often swiftly and completely answered."

Reason should have its place, but not reason alone. It can be the agent of our inclinations. We can find reasons for nearly anything we want to do. We have to distinguish between reason and rationalization. Men have often heard the voice of self when they thought they heard the voice of the Spirit. There are times when it is wise to check our own best judgement with the judgement of others. There are people to whom we can take our problem and ask their counsel. They see it from a different angle, can view the issues more dispassionately and just because they are not personally involved, can be of genuine assistance. Why should we not think of such friends as instruments God can use, just as He uses our own judgement?

Perhaps we had better recognize that the idea of Divine guidance is not always a welcome one. We start life loving to see and choose our path, keen to maintain our independence, resolved to be the masters of our fate and the captains of our souls. Our wills are ours, and we intend to keep them so. Self-will is the hardest thing in existence to surrender to God. When we pray, instead of asking, "What wilt thou have me to do?" what we often say is "This is what I would like to do," and what we want most is approval of the desire. We have all heard of the minister who was called at a higher salary to a church and who spent much time in prayer asking for guidance. His son was stopped in the street and asked what his father was going to do. The boy's reply was, "Father's praying but Mother's packing." It is difficult when asking for guidance to put self and considerations of self out of the reckoning. It takes a long time to learn that our choice in life is a choice of masters, and that only in God's service is there true freedom. It takes a long time to learn that our declarations of independence may land us in real slavery, in subjection to some interest or some object less than the highest. It is a great day in our experience when, with our will surrendered to the Divine Will, we say from the heart, "Lead, kindly Light." It is a great day because we may then expect as never before to discover the guiding hand of God in the every-day experiences of our life.

One of C. E. Montague's stories describes the childhood of a small boy who lived in a very happy home. Every night, just before he dropped off to sleep, this small adventurer murmured to himself his creed, the two words, "Fun tomorrow!" If God is our heavenly Father, we are entitled to adopt a similar attitude to the bigger adventures of adult living. In His Will, said Dante, is our peace. Living by God's guidance we need not be anxious. The fret of toil, the worry about results are taken away. Life becomes an adventure with wonder and romance in it. The future is in God's hands. We do not know what lies round the next turn of the road but He knows. Whatever may confront us His resources will be there and His grace will be sufficient for our need. With this for his confidence a Psalmist wrote: "Trust in the Lord with all thine heart, and lean not unto thine own understanding: In all thy ways acknowledge Him and He shall direct thy paths."

How Does One Learn To Pray?

THE GOSPEL according to Luke tells how the disciples once came upon Jesus when he was praying. They were tremendously impressed by what they saw. Here was a concentration, an absorption, an abandon of which they had no experience. Their prayers, one gathers, were like the prayers of most people—well-intentioned enough but for the most part stereotyped, perfunctory, listless, cold. This was different. This was a revelation of what prayer could be and do. Seeing Jesus on his knees awakened in them a desire to be able to pray—to get past formality and unreality, right into the presence of God, and there pour out one's soul without inhibition or restraint. No sooner had he risen from his knees than one of the disciples, echoing the thought and wish of the others, exclaimed, "Lord, teach us to pray." They saw as they had never done before that prayer was an exercise calling for the development, under tutelage, of proficiency and skill, that it was an art requiring deliberate and sustained cultivation.

If there is to be any substance to our inner life it is a discovery we must all make. Too many of us permit prayer to be a matter not of habit but of instinct. We pray when we are in need, when we are in danger or in a crisis, when we are threatened by the onset of illness or bereavement or failure in business. At such times

we turn to God as instinctively as a hurt or frightened child seeks
the refuge of its mother's arms. So regarded, prayer is the most
rudimentary and characteristic of our life-attitudes, and on its
lower levels it is attended always by two dangers. When we pray
not by fixed habit but by instinct our prayers are apt to be self-
centred. The possibility is that they may never get beyond the
begging stage. Jules Romains observed people in church as they
bowed their heads in silent prayer, asked himself what they were
saying, and surmised that they were presenting such pleas as these:

> O God in heaven, vouchsafe to heal my leg!—
>   to fill my shop with customers.
> Help me to find out if my servant John
> Is robbing me! O God, cure my sore eyes!
> Save me, O God, from being drunk so often!
>
> Lord, let my son pass his examination!
> Help me to make her fall in love with me!
> My God, if only I could get some work!
> My husband makes a martyr of me. Let me die!

The other danger, when prayer follows only the prompting of
instinct, is that it is likely to be spasmodic and occasional. As
soon as the danger is past or the pressure relieved or the sickness
gone the petitioning ceases. In such circumstances what chance
has prayer to grow in depth or range or spirituality? We should be
ashamed if we have literally to be driven to our knees, if the one
thing that drives us there is a crisis, a life situation that has us
licked. That is how it is with most of us. By the constitution of
our nature we are praying creatures, but the instinct to pray is
raw and as uncultivated as it is undisciplined. What percentage
of churchgoers, do you suppose, make a practice of prayer? We
have a voracious appetite for committee work; how is it with us
when we get down on our knees? Some of us have never really
learned to pray. Some of us have forgotten what we learned. Our

trouble is that we are out of touch with God, and if we but realized it, our deepest need is to renew our acquaintance with Him.

How is it to be done? First of all and fundamentally, by recognizing that the praying instinct which is native to each of us waits to be developed from an impulse into an exercise and from an exercise into an art. People complain of their disappointing experiences when they pray. Yet how much of the disappointment is due to the fact that they take for granted that they can become conscious of God at any time, in any mood, with any sort of moral life behind them. They are making a colossal mistake. It is impossible for a man who on his feet is superficial and selfish to become a saint on his knees. The apprehension of God is a moral and spiritual process and calls for purity of heart, singleness of mind, a disciplined will. Prayer is an exercise and an art as well as an instinct. It demands just as much patience, industry and devotion as men give to painting, sculpture or music. Mastery comes only with long practice. Proficiency cannot be picked up in a few short and simple lessons. Brother Lawrence spent ten years teaching himself to pray, ten years of quiet, resolute, unceasing effort. The chief reason why people give up praying is because of the difficulty of prayer, the practical far more than the theoretical difficulty. And back of the practical difficulty lies something deeper. Al Ghazzali, the Moslem mystic, has a sentence that cuts like a knife. "If you are never alone with God, it is not because you are too busy; it is because you don't care for Him, don't like Him. And you had better face the facts." Let us be honest with ourselves about this. Do we really want to learn to pray? Are we prepared to pay the price which mastery of the art involves?

It takes time. At some period in the twenty-four hours a place must be found for it. There are those who favour the morning. It is a matter of principle with them to begin the day with God, to speak with their Maker before they speak with their fellows. The five minutes—it may be no more—spent in recollecting the presence of God and in seeking His blessing and guidance set the tone for the entire day. On the other hand, there are those who favour the evening. They make prayer the last act of the day. By then the house is still, their time is their own, and it is not likely that they will be interrupted. They can pass in review the activities in which they have been engaged and dispose themselves for rest and sleep by beseeching the benediction of God. But whether morning or night or some other period, time must be found for prayer, and if we are in earnest and mean business we shall see that it is systematic and habitual. The fact that we can pray to God at any hour should not make us neglect the duty of drawing near to Him at a self-prescribed hour. The prayer instinct, no less than the hunger instinct, needs to be subject to careful habits of self-discipline. The only way to get beyond impulsive, ejaculatory, spasmodic prayer, prompted in the main by some sort of personal emergency or crisis, is deliberately to cultivate the practice of daily prayer and, like a musician bent on the mastery of his instrument, to refuse to allow anything to interfere with the practice. If we are not prepared to give time to prayer we cannot expect to comprehend its nature or experience its power. Remembering this Lancelot Andrewes demanded of himself: "Do I pray—if not seven times a day, as David, yet at least three times a day as Daniel? If not, as Solomon, at length, yet shortly, as the publican? If not, like Christ, the whole night, at least for one hour? If not on the ground and in ashes, at least not in my bed? O true and self-denying saints of God,—shall we ever be found worthy to touch so much as your shoe-latchet?"

It takes time *and perseverance*. In this as in all the other arts success cannot be achieved unless by dint of persistent application. You listen to a great violinist like Kreisler, and as you watch as well as listen, you see a man in complete command of his instrument, making it speak, putting into music what words are power-less to convey. Did he achieve such skill effortlessly and with ease? No. It is the result of years spent in unremitting toil, toil that must not cease, even for a day, if the skill is to be sustained. And the testimony of the experts is that with prayer it is the same. He who would learn to pray must keep at it, day in day out, year in year out. Many a time he will be tempted to give up but he must resist the temptation with all the strength at his command. He must teach himself to pray whether he feels he wants to pray or not. And when he cannot pray as he knows he should, he must pray as best he can.

When I was a student in Glasgow there was a minister who preached in a church neighbouring the University which was taxed to accommodate the congregations to be found in it twice every Sunday. He was George Morrison of Wellington. More than once on leaving the building I overheard in substance the comment, "The sermon was good but it's the prayer I'll remember." When George Morrison said, "Let us pray," you knew that before long, if you had any spiritual sensitiveness at all, you would be ushered into the Holy of Holies. Yet in the early days of his ministry Morrison's mind was so vagrant and unruly at his private devotions that one night he determined not to get up from his knees till he had not merely repeated, but prayed the Lord's Prayer through, putting real meaning into every one of its clauses. Ten times he made the attempt and ten times he failed. Only at the eleventh attempt did he succeed in praying that short prayer through from start to finish. What perseverance! Said a great saint, "I came at last to this, that I would not rise and go away till I felt I had an audience. And I sometimes felt as sure that I was having an audience as if He had been visibly present before me."

Something that Edison wrote in the twenties is relevant in this connection. "We don't know the millionth part of one per cent about anything. We don't know what water is. We don't know what light is. We don't know what gravitation is. We don't know what enables us to keep on our feet when we stand up. We don't know what electricity is. We don't know what heat is. We don't know anything about magnetism. We have a lot of hypotheses about these things, but that is all. But we do not let our ignorance about all these things deprive us of their use." Apply the logic of that to prayer. It is admittedly a great mystery. It presents us with problems, theoretical and practical, in plenty. But that is no reason why we should not keep on praying. We discover by using. We learn by practice. To know more about the nature of prayer and to experience more of its power the thing to do is, with steady persistence, to keep on praying.

If we are to keep on praying we shall have to widen the range of our prayers. In particular we shall have to get them beyond the begging stage where we are telling God what we want and, as it were, seeking to impose our wills on His, making Him as one writer has expressed it, a sort of celestial valet. I am not suggesting that there should be no element of petition in our prayers. Jesus taught us to pray for things. "Give us this day our daily bread." Could anything be more explicit than that? "If you, being evil, know how to give good gifts to your children, how much more will your heavenly Father give good gifts to those who ask Him?" Nothing could be more explicit than that. The conception of God as our Father makes personal and private petition natural and right but it should not be the dominant element in our prayers. Mark the sequence in the prayer Jesus taught his disciples: "Hallowed be Thy Name. Thy kingdom come. Thy will be done in earth as it is in heaven." Then, but not till then, "Give us this day our daily bread." Note, too, where the stress is placed in the Sermon on the Mount: "Seek ye first the kingdom of God and His righteousness;" "and all these things shall be added unto you." To pray for material things is natural and right but the farther men advance in the School of Prayer the less they do it. One of the Puritans, Thomas Goodwin, says that he knew men who came to God for nothing else but just to come to Him. They scorned to soil themselves with any other errand but just purely to be alone with Him in His Presence.

To get beyond the begging stage in prayer we need to know and practice its other forms. It is far more than petition. It is *confession*—revealing ourselves without reserve to God, making mention of specific sins, sins of thought and motive as well as of word and deed, sins done with a high hand as well as committed unwittingly, and humbly beseeching forgiveness. It is *thanksgiving*— saying grace, as Charles Lamb tells us he was wont to do, not only over meals but over books and flowers and music and friends, praising God for the world in which He has placed us and the work He has given us to do and the truth He has permitted us to learn and all that fills life with zest and adventure. It is *intercession*—lifting hands of prayer not only for ourselves but for those who call us friend, for the Church and the nation and the comity of nations, for needy people and causes everywhere so that the whole round earth is every way bound by gold chains about the feet of God.

Petition, confession, thanksgiving, intercession! Prayer need not be confined to any of these forms. It may simply be thinking about something consciously in the presence of God, as in the case of one who wrote: "Prayer is my Fourth Dimension. When I am alone I cannot think of any theme without bringing in God; and of all the intellectual—not to say spiritual—pleasures my chiefest is to talk with Him." Prayer is any form of intercourse with God; it may be spoken or silent, brief or sustained, a solitary vigil or, as in public worship, a social act, experienced in the heart of the country or amid the roar of a busy street. It is prayer at this deepest level, not necessarily taking form in words but an inner attitude of the soul, the lifting up of the mind to God, which is the secret and stimulus of the best Christian living. It accounts for the tribute Lord Rosebery paid Thomas Chalmers: "Here was a man, bustling, striving, organizing, speaking and preaching with the dust and fire of the world on his clothes, but carrying his shrine with him everywhere."

We think we have no time for prayer. We can make time. We think we have no aptitude for prayer. We can acquire the aptitude. How little we know ourselves or our basic needs! To take the strain from our face and the tension from our nerves, to remove the irritability that makes us unattractive to our family and our associates, to accomplish twice our work in half the time, we need, like Chalmers, to keep a shrine and carry it about with us every-where.

Is the Christian Ideal Attainable?

WHAT ARE we to make of the Sermon on the Mount? There is little disposition anywhere to dispute its moral excellence. Men of every race and creed are ready to acknowledge its loftiness and sublimity. A Jewish scholar has described it as "one of the most wonderful collections of ethical teaching in the world." That reflects the standpoint of many who are not Jews. They will have nothing to do with the Church on its institutional side; they have no interest in theological speculation as to the person or significance of Christ; but they find their hearts strangely warmed by the Sermon on the Mount. In a debate about Christianity Cyril Joad said that he did not care whether Jesus ever existed or whether what the Gospels said about him was true or not. What did seem to him important was the highly original and immensely significant moral teaching which the Gospels contain, for want of attention to which mankind is in a fair way to destroy itself.

With few exceptions people have been willing enough to pay their respects to the excellence of the Sermon on the Mount. When they have criticized it their objections have had to do not with its nobility but with its impracticability. Its very idealism, they have said, is its damaging feature. It is on a plane too exalted for everyday life. It is so far above ordinary conduct that people rarely take it seriously, even Christian people, or when they do take it seriously they find themselves with a divided conscience, if not a besetting hypocrisy. It is strung so high that its most novel and striking features have virtually remained untried and are for the vast majority a dead letter. Excellent, people say, but a kind of poetry, a Utopian dream, beautiful and desirable, but beyond our reach, out of this world, unrelated to the immediate problems of the average man in the workaday world. They agree that there would be an end of all our troubles if people would act in accordance with the teaching of Jesus but, as things are, they see little likelihood of that being done.

Take the injunction, "Love your enemies," which is at the centre of the Sermon on the Mount. What are we to make of that? Reading Dean Inge's diary of the years when he was at St. Paul's Cathedral, London, I came across this entry: "Had a passage of arms with Miss Ruth Fry the Quaker. She wanted to show 'infinite Christian love' towards the Bolsheviks, which is like stroking a tiger on the head and calling him 'poor Puss.' I had just been giving an address to the Quakers whom I love. But in foreign politics their heads are in the clouds." That is where some think Jesus' head was. How, they want to know, can we live by the law of love when the law of force is in the ascendant? If a captain of industry were to run his business, not on competitive lines but on the principle of love, he would soon find himself in the bankruptcy court. If the American nation were to adopt the law of love, were to disband its armies, call its fleets home and dock them, ground all its military planes, concentrate only on the civilian use of atomic energy, set itself to live by the standards of the Sermon on the Mount, what would happen? Nine persons out of ten would answer that were the United States to adopt such a course it would soon become a martyr nation and would lose its status, its trade, its influence, and ultimately its freedom and its soul. The tenth person would answer that the world is waiting for a martyr nation, a nation willing in the cause of right to lose its status and its markets, willing to go to its cross, as Christ went to his, and so lift the world to better things. But in that thoroughgoing, unconventional sense of the word what nation in the world to-day is Christian?

Let us be in no doubt as to what is involved here. To say that the Sermon on the Mount is impracticable is to say that it won't work. Some do not hesitate to come right out and assert just that. That the standard is impossibly high, that as things are, one is bound to be anxious about food and clothing, cannot be absolutely honest, absolutely pure, absolutely loving, cannot forgive seventy times seven or be perfect as God is perfect. About the injunctions—"If any man would go to law with thee, and take away thy coat, let him have thy cloke also"—and, "Give to him that asketh thee, and from him that would borrow of thee turn not thou away," Dr. Lindsay of Balliol College, Oxford, writes: "Most of us are not only not prepared to act like that but quite honestly don't think we ought to act like that." It is a candid sentence and reflects the general standpoint. What the average person wants is a workable moral rule which will afford him clear and reasonable direction in his practical difficulties as an individual and as a citizen. The very perfectionism of the Christian ideal is what makes it seem unattainable.

It is a fact, nonetheless, that Jesus expected his followers to put his teaching into practice. Let me remind you of the specific and categorical terms with which he concluded the Sermon on the Mount. "Everyone who listens to these words of mine and *acts upon them* will be like a sensible man, who built his house on rock. The rain came down, the floods rose, the winds blew and beat upon that house, but it did not fall, for it was founded upon rock.

And everybody who listens to these words of mine and *does not act upon them* will be like a stupid man, who built his house on sand. The rain came down, the floods rose, the winds blew and beat upon that house, and down it fell—with a mighty crash." Nobody who heard those words can have gone away with the impression that he had been confronted with a kind of poetry, a Utopian dream, teaching good but far too good for human nature's daily food. On the contrary, every man knew that he had been challenged there and then to action.

As to that there are two things to remember. The first is that Jesus practiced what he preached. His character is the source and standard of the Christian ideal. The moral principles of Christianity are unique in that they have been personally exemplified. They have been put into operation in the everyday world. Jesus lived what he taught. The trouble with a lot of moral theorizing is that it comes from the pens of arm-chair thinkers. It is when his principles are exemplified in his life that a man earns the moral right to speak, and when he speaks his words have weight and influence That is part of the secret of Jesus. Back of his teaching is his life—illustrating, enhancing, validating everything he said. What he was is still the best commentary on what he taught. Did he urge men to forgive their enemies? How ready he was to forgive. Did he enjoin them to be generous in their judgement of others? Was there ever a more appreciative spirit than his? In the Beatitudes with which the Sermon on the Mount begins he pointed men to the secret of the happy life, and he knew that life at first hand. Have you ever gone through the Beatitudes observing how they each fit perfectly into the framework of his character and life? Surely Henry Drummond was right when he said that Paul wrote I Corinthians 13 having Jesus in mind. Christianity is unique in possessing a teacher who lived what he taught. "Words," wrote Harnack, "effect nothing; it is the power of the personality that stands behind them. He himself stands behind everything that he said."

The other thing to remember is that there have always been followers of Jesus who have sought to practice what he preached. They have refused to regard his teaching as either impracticable or impossible. There are Christians of this persuasion to-day. For them the Sermon on the Mount is not a document of the past. It is a living word for our age and has within it, if we will put it to work, the solution of our problems. Quite as much as Karl Marx's *Das Kapital* it is designed with a view to action. It is to be applied in every region of life—by Christians individually and collectively, in business and politics, in the national and international spheres. To be sure, it makes a heavy demand on human nature, but what ethical teaching worthy of the name does not? The ideal always towers above the actual. It is the function of the moral and religious teacher to hold up the highest conceivable standard and pattern of conduct. The fact that the Christian ideal is so lofty that human nature never actually attains to it does not mean that it is impracticable and irrelevant or that it has to be modified and qualified before it can be serviceable. The Sermon on the Mount is practicable and relevant in the sense in which any ideal is practicable and relevant—as a criterion, a standard, a direction pointer, and especially as a spur, a stimulus a dynamic. It stabs our spirit broad awake. By contrasting what ought to be with what is, it stings us into a consciousness of the obligation under which we stand.

Do you recall the ground on which Gandhi criticized organized Christianity? His complaint was not directed at the Christian ideal—for the Sermon on the Mount he professed admiration again and again—but at the failure of Christians to put it into operation and at their refusal to take it seriously. Stanley Jones once said to him: "Mahatma Gandhi, I am very anxious to see Christianity nationalized in India, so that it shall no longer be a foreign thing identified with a foreign people and a foreign government, but a part of the national life of India and contributing its power to India's uplift and redemption. What would you suggest that we do to make that possible?" This was the reply. "I would suggest, first, that all of you Christians must begin to live more like Jesus Christ. Second, I would suggest that you must practice your religion without adulterating or toning it down. Third, I would suggest that you must put your emphasis upon love, for love is the centre and soul of Christianity."

We are evading the issue where the issue is most pointed and practical if we keep telling ourselves that the Sermon on the Mount is on a plane too exalted for everyday life and, therefore, in any sense unattainable. An ideal which can be quickly and completely fulfilled is not an ideal at all. Browning was thinking of this when he said that "a man's reach should exceed his grasp, or what's a heaven for?" We need ideals to keep us morally on the stretch, to keep us sensitive and conscientious and ardent. And the ideal must be a true ideal, hard, distant, in the final and perfect sense unattainable. Let it ask a mile and a man may produce an inch. Let it ask an inch and a man may not produce even the inch. That an ideal is beyond one's grasp is not a valid criticism against it. That is what every ideal ought to be. But we can strive to come nearer and nearer to it, and through its constraining power a great deal can be accomplished.

If we never attempted anything which we did not expect to do perfectly we should sit with folded hands and never do anything at all. When you started to learn the piano you knew in your heart that you would never be a Paderewski but that did not prevent you from toiling at your scales and five-finger exercises. You have achieved results which you certainly never would have realized if you had decided to do nothing because you could not achieve perfection. It is just the same with the Christian ideal. We may not expect to see it fully realized next year or twenty years hence or in our lifetime, but the world will get nearer to it if we and others of like mind with us do our steady best to approximate to it and to translate as much of it as we can into reality.

> Far is the time, remote from human sight,
> When war and discord on the earth shall cease,
> Yet every prayer for universal peace
> Avails that blessed time to expedite.

The Sermon on the Mount makes a very heavy demand on us. We may never be able to rise to all that it requires but we ought to be endeavouring to work it into our hearts and lives. Are we really trying to live like Jesus Christ? Are we practicing our religion without adulterating or toning it down? Where are we putting the emphasis in our daily living—on competition, on force, or on love which is the centre and soul of Christianity? It just won't do for a Christian to say that his business or his politics can't be run on the lines of the Sermon on the Mount and leave it at that. If we are not prepared right up to the limit of our capacity to follow what we admit to be the teaching of Christ, what right have we to call ourselves Christians at all?

I speak for myself, but I imagine that I am also speaking for you, when I say that the trouble is that we are living by standards that are far too low. We look at the Sermon on the Mount and at its stern injunctions and what do we do? We regard it as a rather remote ideal which should have some effect on our conduct but not very much because deep down we feel that we cannot live up to it. Then, regarding it as a remote and irrelevant ideal, we incline to fold our hands and settle down complacently in the customary, conventional ways, barely a whit different from men and women who never darken the door of a church or make any pretence at professing the Christian name. It won't do. It just won't do. If we have any intention of taking our religion seriously, if the mind of Jesus is to be our guiding star, we must take the moral principles of Jesus, and relying on God for help and grace, endeavour to work them into our hearts and lives and into the heart and life of the world.

"Begin to live more like Jesus Christ . . . practice your religion without adulterating or toning it down . . . put your emphasis upon love, for love is the centre and soul of Christianity." And remember this. The Christian ideal, put into practice, can work like a ferment. Once before it turned the world upside down, or as Chesterton phrased it, turned the world right side up, and it can do it again. When men really set themselves to translate the moral principles of Jesus into action they make an impact on society which lifts the whole level and tone of its life. Their own lives become focal-points of God's grace through which society is transformed. They help to hasten the coming of the Kingdom of God.

Why Did Jesus Die?

W HY DID Jesus die? He needn't have done, at any rate not
when he did, in the thirty-third year of his life. He might
have stayed by the carpenter's bench at Nazareth. He might have
refrained from stirring up a hornet's nest about his ears. If only
he had been content to hold his tongue, if only he had been prepared to compromise a little, if only he had let the powers that be
alone, instead of poking fun at them as trumpet blowers and blind
leaders of the blind, instead of castigating them as foxes, hypocrites
and whited sepulchres, he might have lived to be as white haired as
Caiaphas, or as elderly as any of the Scribes and Pharisees respons-
ible for having him handed over to Pilate.

Why did he do what he did? Why did he adopt and resolutely
maintain an attitude that made it certain his life would be taken?
Why did he go on teaching truths obnoxious to those in authority
after they had made it plain as a pike staff that they would not
tolerate him one moment longer than they could possibly help?
One thing is beyond dispute. He was labouring under no illusions. It will not do to write him down as a mystic and visionary,
out of touch with the situation, completely taken aback when the
officers came out with staves and torches to arrest him. In one sense
of the word, he was a realist. He saw how things were developing.

Early in his ministry the shadow of the Cross fell athwart his path. Nevertheless, he did what he did with extreme deliberation. That is the whole point in the testimony of the Evangelist—"He steadfastly set his face to go to Jerusalem," though nobody knew better than he did what awaited him there. He chose the Cross. He died as so few men do—voluntarily. "I lay down my life of myself," he once said. "No one taketh it away from me. I have power to lay it down and I have power to take it again." It is no exaggeration to say that Jesus saw everything in his own life, yes and everything in the life of the world, everything in history, leading up to and culminating in his death.

Why, then, did he die? That is a constantly recurring question. For those who treat the New Testament seriously it is an inevitable question. In generation after generation it has engaged men's minds. You could stock a small library with the books written on it. There was once a man, however, who gave an agony of thought to this question. He did what Luther says we should all do, he began his thinking "at the wounds of Christ." And here was the conclusion he reached, a surprisingly simple and straight-forward conclusion if one has regard to the complexity of the issues involved: "He died for all, that they which live should not henceforth live unto themselves but unto him who died for them."

For some of us that may be a new angle from which to view what happened at Calvary. I hasten to add that it is only one angle. There are others, many others, but as a rule they receive more attention than this one. We are accustomed to think of the Cross in terms of forgiveness and reconciliation and new-found sources of moral power; and we have every right to do so, for behind all such thought there is the explicit teaching of the New Testament, and not only the explicit teaching of the New Testament but the radiant, transformed lives of men and women in every Christian generation. But the death of Jesus not only means that something amazing and wonderful has been done for us; it means that something demanding and exacting is expected of us. Christ on the Cross is a perpetual challenge to our world, and the head and front of the challenge is that we give up self-centred living. To avert our eyes from the Cross, to refuse to take up the challenge that confronts us there, is to proclaim ourselves devoid of two qualities for the want of which our civilization finds itself even now under sentence of decline and decay—the qualities of feeling and honour.

Where in such matters as these do we stand? If the facts are to be frankly faced and recognized, and the whole truth told, do we not stand condemned, you and I and all of us? Most of us live for ourselves, if not all the time, at any rate for by far the greater part of it. The chief librarian at Dagenham, England, recently investigated the history of an area on which there now stands an immense Ford factory. One of the first purchasers of the site was a certain John Ward, a member of Parliament, who bought it when it was flooded and therefore cheap, and then had a Bill passed to drain it at the public expense. After his death there was found among his papers this extraordinary prayer: "O Lord, Thou knowest I have mine estates in the City of London, and likewise that I have recently purchased an estate in fee simple in the County of Essex. I beseech Thee to preserve the two counties of Middlesex and Essex from fire and earthquake, and as I have a mortgage in Hertfordshire, I beg of Thee likewise to have an eye of compassion on that county; for the rest of the counties, Thou mayest deal with them as Thou art pleased." I hope I am not a malicious person, but it affords me a good deal of quiet satisfaction to inform you that Ward died in a debtor's prison, and the fact that he died there does not shake in the least my confidence in the efficacy of prayer.

We smile at Ward and his canting prayer, but can we really afford to? Is there not something there that, as Coleridge would say, "finds" us? When Gogol's play, *Inspector General*, was given its first public performance the audience laughed to the point of tears at it; it was such a humorous exposure of the complicated corruption of old Russia. But suddenly from the wings there was a voice, it was the voice of the dramatist himself! "What are you laughing at? You are laughing at yourselves." Whereupon, we are told, there was silence—and real tears. And so with poor John Ward, M.P. Nobody nowadays would dream of composing a prayer like his, but why? Because our motives are so different from his, or because we are less naïve, more subtle and sophisticated? What are our master motives? What are we living for? What sort of dominant demand are we making upon life? And what is prayer but the dominant demand of one's life? Can we truthfully say that we are not like Ward, that we do not habitually and chronically think in terms of self, security, position, comfort, but that as a matter of fixed principle and long-established habit God and our neighbour come first?

Some people defend themselves against the charge that they are self-centred. They claim that they have long since surrendered personal ambition. They no longer live for themselves; if they live for anybody it is for their children. But living for one's children may simply be another form of living for self. Family love, family affection can be a terribly possessive and selfish thing, as when a mother like Salome wishes her sons to outdistance in achievement and social standing the children of her friends and neighbours. One frequently sees in the hopes which parents cherish for their children a reflection of their own frustrated desires and ambitions. This can be a fine and beautiful thing, as when David, forbidden himself to build a temple to God, makes it possible for his son to do so, but it can also be an unattractive and ugly thing. So much depends on the nature of the hopes we cherish for our children. That a son should build a temple to the most high God, that he should be a minister of God, that he should devote his life to some high and worthy, even if materially unrewarding end, that is splendid and noble. That he should have a good living, every material comfort, an accepted place in the best circles, what in God's name and in the light of Christ's standards of value is that?

Nepotism is an ugly word and all its associations are ugly. It forgets completely the dictum of our Lord that "A man's true life does not consist of the abundance of the things he possesses." Some time ago a woman said to me, when we were talking about recruits for the Christian ministry, "I would never dream of putting any son of mine into the ministry; it doesn't offer a decent living to anybody." So often it is when it is too late to make use of it that the apt rejoinder occurs to me. I know now that I should have reminded that woman of something that was said by Dr. Goodwin, the first president of Harvard University: "God had only one son, and he was a minister."

There are people who are prepared to defend self-centred living. As an undergraduate at Glasgow University I listened to the then Earl of Birkenhead, the newly appointed Lord Rector, while he extolled self-interest as the mainspring of human conduct. I think I can hear him yet as he declared—"The world still has glittering prizes to offer to those who have stout hearts and sharp swords." There we were, well over three thousand of us, young, keen, idealists, and that was what he chose to say to us. When you come to think of it, it was substantially the thing that Hitler said to the young men of Germany. It is popular doctrine. Nor is it confined to totalitarian regimes. In a world like this, you will hear men say, if you don't look after yourself, your family, your immediate personal interests, who will? If you don't join the money-making scramble and fight for a place in the sun, you will be left out in the cold. Consciously or unconsciously, that is the working philosophy of thousands upon thousands of people, of people inside as well

as outside the churches. In its crudest form it finds expression in
the old cynical saying—Every man for himself and the devil take
the hindmost.

But that is the law of the jungle. It is the doctrine of the survival of the fittest. It means subscription to the view that the race
of life is to the swift and the battle to the strong. It involves in the
final analysis the establishment and maintenance of the competitive principle and the rejection of the co-operative one. Moreover,
if Paul is to be believed, it was precisely this sort of thing that
Jesus died to put a stop to. "He died for all that they which live
should not henceforth live unto themselves but unto him who
died for them." And isn't it high time it was being stopped? It
is surely apparent to every thinking person that self-interest as a
working philosophy of life has broken down. Self-centred living
is at the root of practically all the evil and misery in the world.

No home can be built on such a foundation. When a husband
lives for himself, thinks only of himself, considers none save himself, he may have a fine house but he is forever debarred from
having a happy home. And similarly with a wife, a son, a daughter.
The people who ruin home life are the people who make it re-
volve about themselves, who forget that marriage and family
life are a friendly partnership, a joyous adventure in mutual
co-operation.

And as with family life, so with national and international life.
In a world like ours, a world in which space has been annihilated
and the peoples brought uncomfortably close to one another by
means of the radio and the aëroplane and the atomic bomb, no nation can any longer live unto itself. Isolationism as a political concept is as dead as the dodo. Yet the irony of the situation is that
isolationism is still a potent force. The nations are finding it hard
to give up living for themselves. For so long the motto of nations,
as well as of men, has been not Each for All but Each for Self. We

were so slow—I am thinking now of the democratic peoples—to unite even in self-defence. If we had combined against Hitler in the middle thirties, it would have been a comparatively simple matter to deal with him. Turkey's position all through World War II was the common position up to 1939—self-interest dominating every major move in the field of foreign affairs. And even when you have co-operation among nations, how often for its governing factor is it motivated by self-interest? Do you recall after the Russo-German pact how Russia was the enemy and Stalin was featured in cartoon after cartoon as a bear? Then, when she came over to our side, Russia became a friend and Stalin a hero. Now the process is in reverse. The axis, the democratic bloc, the united front are apt basically to be devices to guarantee security.

Take another instance. Before World War II, the gospel of economic nationalism was preached practically on every continent. "Let the nation be a self-sufficient unit" was the slogan everywhere. But with nation after nation pursuing that policy, living for itself, what happened? Well do we know what happened. With our own eyes we saw what happened. World depression set in; world trade dried up; the cry arose, "We need colonies, access to raw materials, a market for our goods." There was no end of competition, friction, animosity. For years we had powder-heaps lying all over the place and sparks flying in every conceivable direction. In 1939 war came, the second global war in one generation, and no one can possibly deny that one of its causes was the absence of co-operation, the foolish determination of the nations to live unto themselves.

"Is it true," some one asked, "that all the people in the world could get into the State of Texas?" "Yes," was the answer, "if they were friends." Increase of contacts demands increase of friendliness. "People," writes Dr. Fosdick, "sneer at love as a weak sentiment, as a luxury. Love is not a luxury. It is the profoundest practical need of mankind. On no other terms can human life sustain the mutual relationships into which, by its very nature, it is compressed."

But from the international issue let us return to the personal one. When all is said and done the most effective way in which we can help to set the world right is to be set right ourselves. Are we self-centred? Is self-interest the mainspring of our conduct? Nothing could be more unchristian. The life and death and principles of Jesus are diametrically opposed to the sentiment that the world has glittering prizes to offer to those who have stout hearts and sharp swords. The Sermon on the Mount and the Cross confront us with a wholly different scale of values.

"If you want to know," says Dr. Inge, "what you really believe, ask yourself two questions. First, if I had a fairy godmother who promised to grant me three wishes, what would those wishes be? And second, what are the things, if any, that I would die rather than do?" Those two questions are worth thinking over. They can best be reviewed in the light of Paul's great saying, "He died for all that they which live should not henceforth live unto themselves but unto him who died for them."

Where Can We Find Security?

J UNG maintains that one of the primary needs of man is to feel secure. How much of our talk nowadays is about that very thing—family security, social security, national security, collective security. Can you think of anything our generation is seeking more? We want security against poverty, against sickness, against unemployment, against old age, against war. Life in the twentieth century is a risky business. As far as productive capacity is concerned we could all be thinking in terms of abundance. Instead what we are thinking of is survival.

This is a craving common at each stage of life—childhood, adolescence, the middle years, old age. It shows itself in every individual as he grows up, sometimes in fear, sometimes in indolence, sometimes in unwillingness, because of the risks involved, to come to grips with life and shoulder responsibility. *Peter Pan* and *Mary Rose* are not extravagant whimsicalities. There is an uncannily accurate reading of one side of human nature in them both, uncannily accurate perhaps because Barrie put so much self-portraiture into them. All the way through life we are beset by a deep longing for security, for four walls and a fireside, for a cozy corner and an arm-chair and a pair of slippers.

Here and there one comes across complaints that the craving

for security is sapping the spirit of this nation. Hanson Baldwin thinks that because of it the pioneer psychology has given way to soft living, and that we are so taken up with collective security that we are forgetting to stress the case for individual initiative. Sir Oliver Franks, the British Ambassador at Washington, was warning us not long ago to be on our guard against establishing a society which mistakes comfort for civilization. It is a real danger. You must have noticed how the advertisers in our newspapers never weary of commending their wares as conducive to easy living. Nothing is praised so much as ease—easy work, easy play. And the idea has taken hold. What schoolboy would prefer a difficult exercise to a simple one? What workman would ask for a hard job rather than a soft one? What preacher would deliberately elect a down-town charge in preference to a residential one? We live in an age which in its craving for security sees ease and comfort as goals to be pursued, and difficulty and hardship as evils to be avoided. What it overlooks is that strength of character, national and personal, can only be gained by roughing it, by facing odds and being disciplined by life. Can you have courage without danger? Can you have sympathy without suffering? Can you have tenderness without weakness or pain?

Even in religion we see the tendency. The only thing that multitudes seek from religion is security. In Maxwell Anderson's play *High Tor* there is a scene in which two men, Biggs and Skimmerhorn, find themselves in a position of grave danger. Their conversation runs thus:

> Biggs: Say, do you know any prayers?
> Skimmerhorn: I know one.
> Biggs: Say it, will you?
> Skimmerhorn: Matthew, Mark, Luke and John,
>   Bless the bed that I lie on.
> Biggs: That's not much good, that one.
> Skimmerhorn: It's the only one I know.

There is no easing of the danger and the men resume conversation.

> Skimmerhorn: I don't know how to pray. (A crash)
> Biggs (on his knees): O God, I never did this before
> and I don't know how, but keep me safe here and I'll be
> a better man. I'll put candles on the altar, yes, I'll
> get that Spring Valley Church fixed up, the one that's
> falling down. I can do a lot for you if you let me live.
> O God—

Is there exaggeration in that? Some perhaps, but not much. There are people who turn to religion only because of what it can do for them—provide an escape from worry, from sleeplessness, from fatigue; furnish them with ability to stand up to life, to make a success of it, to extract from it the maximum amount of happiness. To have recourse to religion, however, for no other reason than the service it can render us is to exploit it. Not only can it do great things for us; it expects great things from us. If anyone makes the point that Christ habitually offered men security in the sense of interior peace and adequacy for life, it has to be added that he never stopped there, and he rarely began there. He was always emphasizing and reiterating the cost of discipleship. "Strait is the gate" and "narrow is the way" and "few there be that find it" was what he said.

As to that Dr. Luccock of Yale has some pertinent remarks to which the widest publicity might profitably be given. "In this day of psychology of all brands, good, almost good, and charlatan, the business of not worrying has been elevated into a national cult. The magic word is 'Relax.' Many ministers have discovered that word 'relax' and have compressed the whole Gospel into it. They are almost on the verge of rewriting the Scriptures to read, 'If any man will come after me, let him relax' or 'Go ye into all the world and keep down your blood pressure.' "

Security is a great boon and in one form or another we all

crave it and are actively seeking it, but it is not the highest good. Let us be very clear about that. Not that we should be kept safe but that we should be kept loyal, ought to be our prayer. For security some have paid far too great a price. They have supposed it could be obtained by *closing their minds*. John Henry Newman is an example. He was a rarely gifted personality, a profoundly religious soul, but he had an intellect that was essentially sceptical. What was he to do? Was he, like Socrates, to follow the argument wherever it might lead *or*—for, as he saw it, this was the alternative—yield unquestioning obedience to Mother Church? In the end he adopted the latter course. He sought the shelter of Rome. He retired within four walls and tried to persuade himself that he had reached journey's end. There are many like him. They have welcomed security even though it meant complete submission to authority. Millions did it in the case of Hitler. Millions are doing it in the U.S.S.R. T. H. Huxley once expressed the wish to be wound up like a clock every morning. The attraction of a mechanistic philosophy, of an unalterable creed, that will relieve us of responsibility is born of this desire. It becomes strong in the forties and grows stronger as each decade passes. We like to jog along in the old and well-worn ruts and are happy if we are left undisturbed. We are instinctively hostile to change; we fear it as though it were somehow subversive; we labour under the illusion that security is dependent on the absence of change, on the preservation of the *status quo*. It is an illusion because, as Emerson put it, God offers us a choice between truth and ease. We cannot have both. Nothing is static in this world. Our values, our beliefs, our great, historic conceptions of freedom and democracy must be reinterpreted from generation to generation. There is no real security in facing the contingencies of life with a closed mind. What do you suppose Unamuno meant by concluding his book on *The Tragic Sense of*

Life with the sentence, "May God deny you peace but give you glory"?

For the sake of security some *surrender their ideals.* They do what we all incline to do; they think of money and its acquisition as essential to security. It is the prime necessity. They have endless faith in it and in its omnipotence. What will men not do for money? The desire of gaining it and the fear of losing it are our chief breeders and propagators of cowardice and corruption. For money men will compromise with honour and principle, keep silent when they should speak out, engage in sharp practices; for money mothers will constrain their daughters into loveless marriages; for money there are those who will sell their bodies and souls. The temptation is not one that besets a few. It assumes a great variety of forms and in one fashion or another keeps plaguing us all. To resist it we need to take high ground. We need to have standards of conduct and behaviour which no pressure, financial or otherwise, can lower. We need to fortify our souls as Carlyle did: "Truth! though the heavens crush me for following. No False-hood! though a whole celestial Lubberland were the price of Apostasy." Not to be kept safe but to be kept loyal should be our prayer.

For the sake of security some *slip out from under their duties and obligations.* They take no active, personal part as citizens or churchmen in the tasks that confront our troubled generation but turn away from it and dodge all dodgable responsibilites. They seek to escape when they should ask for strength to hold their ground, to serve the common good, to believe in man and his future, to work for both, no matter how many or grievous the set-backs. The road to the better world is going to be a long, rough, uphill road. To travel it is going to test our reserves of per-severance, courage and conviction. "We all thought," said Richard Baxter about England's Civil War, "that one battle would end it, but we were all very much mistaken." We, too, had our hopes of a better era when Hitler and Mussolini and the Japanese war lords met defeat. We see now that our diagnosis of our predicament was too superficial. We still have a battle on our hands and will have for many a year to come. This is no time to be dodging our obligations. This is no time to give up our hopes of a better world or to contract out of our responsibility for seeing to it that those hopes take real shape. Security can be bought at too great a price. It will never be ours if we make criticism a substitute for action, if we grumble about corruption but leave the corrupting agencies unmolested, if we do no more than grumble. That's the low road. Don't take it. Take the high road. Assert with Henry Newbolt:

> Once again with proud hearts we make the old surrender,
> Once again with high hearts serve the age to be,
> Not for us the warm life of Earth, secure and tender,
> Ours the eternal wandering and warfare of the sea.

The great souls of the world have not thought of security as the highest good. They have not looked on life as their own, given to them to further their own ends, to enable them to push their fortunes and have a good time. They have not asked for exemption or immunity from the battle or to be sheltered from its dangers and difficulties. "By faith Abraham, when he was called to go out into a place which he should afterwards receive for an inheritance, obeyed; and he went out, not knowing whither he went." Security was not the first consideration with the Father of the Faithful. Nor, to take a very different case, was it with Socrates. Do you remember his speech to his judges at his trial?

> If you were to say to me, "Socrates, this time we will let you go,
> but on this condition, that you cease from carrying on this search
> of yours, and from philosophy; if you are found following these

pursuits again, you shall die"; I say, if you offered to let me go on these terms, I should reply, "Athenians, I hold you in the highest regard and love, but I will obey God rather than you; and as long as I have breath and strength I will not cease from philosophy, and from exhorting you, and declaring the truth to every one of you whom I meet, saying as I am wont, 'You are a citizen of Athens, a city which is very great and very famous for wisdom and power of mind. Are you not ashamed of caring so much for the making of money, and for reputation? Will you not think or care about wisdom, and truth, and the perfection of your soul?' And, therefore, Athenians, either acquit me or do not acquit me; but be sure that I shall not alter my way of life; no, not if I have to die for it many times."

In every age and among all religions God has had gallant servants of the common good who have lived in scorn of circumstance, who have put truth and justice and principle first regardless of the cost to themselves, who have died in faith, not having received the promises, but with their faces turned in the direction of the promises, and sure of the ultimate vindication and fulfilment of the promises. John Masefield was thinking of that great and honourable company when he wrote:

> Not for us are content, and quiet, and peace of mind,
> For we go seeking a city that we shall never find.
>   · · ·
> Only the road, and the dawn, the sun, the wind,
>   and the rain,
> And the watch fires under the stars, and sleep,
>   and the road again.
>   · · ·
> We travel the dusty road, till the light of the day
>   is dim,
> And sunset shows us its spires, away on the world's rim.
>   · · ·

Yes, all through life we crave security, long for four walls and a fireside, for a cozy corner and an arm-chair and a pair of slippers.

But where has God had his dealings with men? By the fireside? Open your Bible and what do you find? It is on the wind-swept hill that the bush burns. It is on Sinai, amid thunder and lightning, that the word is spoken and the command given. It is on a stony pillow that men have dreamed of the ladder of communication between earth and heaven. Not when all was going well with them but when they were up against odds, contending against adversaries without and within has God come mightily in renewal of life to men. Which perchance explains the prayer entry in George Whitefield's *Journal*: "When Thou seest me in danger of nestling,—in pity—in tender pity—put a thorn in my nest to prevent me from it."

Where is the final security? Is it in lands or houses or bonds in the bank? It is not. Is it in tanks, aircraft carriers, atomic bombs? It is not. Then where is it? It is in our faith in God. It is in our experience of God. It is in the way of life that results from such faith and experience. Everything that is of value is secure in Him. Said John Newton, "If you think you see the ark of the Lord falling, you can be quite sure that that is due to a swimming in your own head." If the work we do and the words we say are in line with the eternal purposes, they will stand. And the eternal purposes, not our comfort, are what matter most. Arthur Hugh Clough wrote:

> It fortifies my soul to know
> That, though I perish, truth is so:
> That, howso'er I stray and range,
> Whate'er I do, Thou dost not change.
> I steadier step when I recall
> That, if I slip, Thou dost not fall.

With this for our confidence we can meet and match our times. We can take the high road and gird ourselves for a conflict whose issue is sure. "This is the victory that overcometh the world, even our faith."

What Makes a Church Vital?

RECENTLY in Britain a prominent minister with whom I was discussing the state of religion in the country at large surprised me by saying, "The Church of England is dead, the Church of Scotland is dying." Looking back on the conversation I am sure that he did not mean me to take what he said literally. As I see it now, he was deliberately going out of his way to describe the current situation in arresting and alarming terms. He was anxious that I should appreciate how serious and critical it was. He knew, as we all do, that generalizations are to be avoided; they are as a rule too arbitrary; they are seldom comprehensive enough to cover all the facts. If he committed himself to a sweeping generalization it was because he wanted to bring home to me the plight and predicament of the British churches. He went on to speak at length about such matters as the decline in church attendance, the apathy of the rank and file of church members, the want of initiative and resource—even of competence—on the part of ministers, and the decreasing influence of the churches in national and international affairs. Many a time since we talked together, his deliberately provocative sentence has come back to mind: "The Church of England is dead, the Church of Scotland is dying."

It should be remembered that for men to talk so about the

Church is not new. In generation after generation there have been those who have dogmatically predicted its gradual decline and ultimate decease, though every time the deceased has proved too lively for the obsequies. When I was in the final year at the Divinity School in Glasgow, a minister came up from London to address the outgoing class. To this day I cannot make out why he was chosen to address us. He assured us that nation-wide the trend was such that in ten years' time churches all over the country would be closing their doors, and in his case there could be no doubt that he meant literally every word he said. His bearing and demeanour indicated as much; he had the look of a beaten man. He was a false prophet. Not ten but twenty years have passed since he made his gloomy predictions, and while in many quarters church life in Britain may be in the doldrums, the churches are not closing their doors, or if by reason of the shifting population they are closed in one area they are soon opened in another. The Church is an institution that never goes out of business. Subjected through the centuries to calumny, opposition, persecution, never an infallible institution, its representatives not what they ought to be, the assaults upon it from within sometimes greater, certainly more insidious, than those from without, its survival is one of the wonders of the world. Its continued existence and persistence for sixty generations is sheer miracle. "Sire," said Theodore Beza to King Henry of Navarre, "it belongs in truth to the Church of God, in the name of which I speak, to receive blows and never to give them, but it will please your Majesty to remember that the Church is an anvil that has worn out many a hammer."

There is a sentiment to match with the one I heard expressed in Britain. We do well to give good heed to both. We work on an enduring institution. There is no likelihood of its disappearance or decease. But anyone who knows, even in outline, the story of the Church is aware that its course has been a chequered one

and that if it has had periods of strength, it has not been unfamiliar with periods of weakness. There have been times, stirring
times, when it has been a potent, pervasive, dynamic influence,
when, as Jesus predicted would be the case, it has served like salt
and light and leaven—making character, shaping thought, con-
trolling events, influencing for good the designs and destinies of
nations. There have been other times when its power has palpably
dwindled and its influence shrunk, when it has been well-nigh
moribund, affording neither light nor leading, with no prophetic
voices to stir and challenge its own or the public conscience,
without vitality or vision or gifts of leadership, having a name to
live, yet at the point of death.

In the periods of its strength, its peak periods, what have been
the marks of the Church, its outstanding features, the qualities
in its life and in its members that have caught the eye and held as
well as attracted attention? Henry Ward Beecher commenced his
ministry, as most preachers do, in a mood of optimism and elation.
He expected to elicit a ready response from his hearers and to see
interest in the work of the church growing and deepening. His
hopes did not materialize; months passed and there was no per-
ceptible stirring anywhere in the congregation; everything went
on in ordinary, commonplace, uneventful fashion. He was at his
wit's end and plagued with depression when one day the thought
seized him: "There was a reason why, when the Apostles preached
they succeeded, and I will find it out if it is to be found out."
From that moment he was on the right track. It is the same sort of
strategy I have in mind when I suggest that it should be a rewarding exercise for us to look at the Church in the periods of its
strength and note what were then its most striking characteristics.

Take, for instance, *the sense of conviction*. That has all along
been one of the marks of a living Church. Whether in the first
century or the sixteenth or the twentieth it has owed its vitality

to the fact that its members have had a personal experience of Jesus Christ and have found in him and in his gospel a new interest in life, a master motive, a centre for thought, an incentive to action. If they have been clear when others have been confused, absorbed when others have been distracted, confident when others in bewilderment have vacillated from one goal to another and from one interest to another, it is because they have discovered a star to steer by, a cause, a creed, a passionate attachment. No matter to what source you turn, and the sources are as varied as they are numerous—the letters of Paul, the Confessions of Augustine, the sermons of Luther, the hymns of Wesley, the theology of Schleiermacher, the biography of Elizabeth Fry, the autobiography of Grenfell of Labrador—you encounter people about whom the last thing to say is that they are dealing with propositions in the air or relying on rumour and hearsay. On the contrary, they are building on the proved facts of their own experience. They are speaking at first hand. They have deep and thoroughgoing convictions, convictions that have spurred them to action, involved them in repeated self-sacrifice, and made ardent propagandists of every one of them. Suppose in this regard we do what Beecher did and go back for a criterion to the Apostles. "I know whom I have believed," says Paul, and for him that is the fundamental matter from which everything stems. "It is no cunningly devised fables we are giving you," says Peter, "for we were eye witnesses of Christ's majesty," and you can sense that having said that the man feels that for him there is no more direct, no more immediate court of appeal to which to turn. In the case of the Apostle John, the stress is the same: "It is of what we have heard, of what we have seen with our eyes, of what we watched reverently and touched with our hands—it is about the Word who is the life that we are now writing." Who can fail to detect the note of conviction in those words, the glowing certainty, the intoxicating enthusiasm?

Those are qualities of which the Church stands in urgent need to-day. The contention of Berdyaev, the Russian theologian, is incontrovertible: "There is no longer any room in the world for a merely external form of Christianity, based upon custom. The world is entering upon a period of catastrophe and crisis, when we are being forced to take sides, and in which a higher and more intense kind of spiritual life will be demanded of Christians." Yet the dearth of robust conviction in the Church is unmistakable. Where the fundamentals of the Christian religion are concerned there is among its members an alarming amount of vague and woolly thinking. To great numbers of them it has come to mean hardly anything more than being kind and neighbourly and doing good as opportunity arises—which is well enough in its way and which was never more needed than now, but it is certainly not basic Christianity. For Protestantism in America, despite a steady increase in church membership and vastly improved opportunities of religious education, religious illiteracy—the words are not too strong—constitutes a first-class problem: multitudes uninformed and misinformed, lost in a wilderness of *laissez-faire* thinking, having broken with the beliefs of an earlier day, with nothing to put in their place, at any rate nothing as positive and vital, so that when they are asked what they believe, they fall back on impressions absorbed in childhood or repeat vague generalities rather than offer anything in the nature of a clear-cut credo. Here are the replies of three persons classing themselves as Christians, to the question, Do you believe there is a God? "Oh, yes, I believe there is. But whether I have just been brought up to believe it as a child, I don't know." "Well, I've always been brought up to believe, but you do wonder sometimes. I don't think I can argue on it." "I couldn't say, we are only told there is one, and I suppose we must believe in one."

What such vagueness means for active, intelligent, mature

church membership is only too obvious. It turns out men and women who have no star to steer by, no centre for thought, no incentive to action. They have no creed, no passionate attachment which wakens their enthusiasm, rouses their devotion and loyalty, and sweeps them off their feet. As another has put it: "They have a pew in some church and if it is not too fine, or again not too wet, they will be there. No one can say they are against Jesus Christ. It would be just not true. But on the other hand, they are not hot for him, not absorbed in his cause, not enthusiastic to help him, not almost one-idead about this thing as many people are about football, or art, or business, or whatever makes life for them. Always when they speak of him it is with grave respect; often they do a little for him; but nothing that spells sacrifice, that pushes them out from the centre of their lives, that upsets their own comforts, that means giving up anything they really want. They are mildly Christian, but not very much." Isn't that the story of most of us?

> What would I burn for, and whom not spare?
> I who have faith in an easy chair.

And it all runs back in the final case to the absence in us of the quality so apparent in Christians in every forward-moving epoch of the Church's history—the absence of personal conviction, rooted and grounded in immediate, self-authenticating experience.

All of which brings me to another mark of a living Church. A sense of conviction always issues *in a sense of vocation*. Whoever genuinely believes anything becomes a propagandist. If you believe a certain medicine is effective, you will make it your business to recommend it to others. If you believe a certain political theory, practically applied, is likely to work out for the greatest happiness of the greatest number, and the belief and the welfare of humanity really count for something with you, then you will conceive it to be your first task to win others to its support. Whatever you may think of the content of Peter Howard's book you cannot question the aptness and soundness of its title—*Ideas Have Legs*. Indeed they have—long, strong legs. See to what lengths they carried Hitler and the German people, with the whole world in consequence involved in a maelstrom. See what a revolution they are working in Russia, and not only in Russia but far beyond it, for Communism is the most aggressive missionary movement of our time. Its representatives have made the world their parish and display a devotion, a venturesomeness, a courage that compel self-examination. Said Radek, at one time the chief of propaganda in Moscow, "This Communism, you see, is a religion. Our young men must preach its gospel. They are willing to die for it." There you have the very thing for which I am pleading—a sense of conviction issuing in a sense of vocation.

At its best, Christianity has always had it. "Necessity is laid upon me, yea woe is unto me if I preach not the gospel." It is the cry that accounts for the missionary journeys of Paul and the establishment of the Church in Asia Minor and Europe. "Here I stand: I can no other." It is the declaration of Luther at the Diet of Worms—daring, defiant, uncompromising, final: the declaration of a man with a tremendous sense of mission. "I will not be a liar. I will speak in season and out of season. I will not take counsel with flesh and blood, and flatter myself with the dream that, while every man on earth back to Abel who ever tried to testify against the world has been laughed at, misunderstood, slandered, and that—bitterest of all—by the very people he loved, I am alone to escape. My path is clear and I will follow in it. He who died for me and who gave me you, shall I not trust him through whatever new and strange paths he may lead me?" It is Charles Kingsley's letter to his wife when his forthright teaching and preaching involved him in a turmoil of bitter controversy and strife and when friends and relatives pleaded with him to "put the tongue of discretion in the cheek of propriety." There is tension in it, too much tension. It would have helped Kingsley if he could have relaxed more than he did. But the strength of conviction and the sense of mission leap at us from every sentence.

Ideas have legs. The fires that kindled the heroes of the Faith, the thing that churned their souls and kept them toiling on in the teeth of obstacles, apparently insuperable, was an idea, nay rather an ideal, an ideal which had become incarnate in Christ. It gave them a cause in which they fervently believed and which sent them out in joyous and deliberate abandon as on a crusade. In 1830 Benjamin Constant, the French philosopher, received a message at the hands of his friends in Paris who were over-throwing the Bourbons. "A terrible game is being played here: our heads are in danger: come and add yours." That was the appeal of Christ to his followers. What we need in the Church now is the same crusading spirit for, to quote Berdyaev once more, these are times when "Christianity is going back to the state she enjoyed before Constantine; she has to undertake the conquest of the world afresh." She will never do it unless her members are animated by a devotion to their cause no less passionate than Hitler felt for his and the Communists feel for theirs. She will never do it until she is less timid, cautious and compromising and far more venturesome and aggressive. She will never do it until her leaders, instead of drawing up pious, platitudinous resolu-tions about which everybody can agree, go in for courageous thinking and plain, candid speaking. She will never do it until the rank and file of her members know what they believe and why, and have for their master motive the dissemination of their faith the world over.

Years ago in Boston Bishop F. J. McConnell delivered a speech, the memory of which is still treasured. "During the Boxer

Rebellion," he said, "hundreds, probably thousands of Chinese Christians were martyred. There they knelt, with their heads on the blocks, the knives trembling in the hands of their executioners. All they needed to do was to grunt out a Chinese word that meant 'I recant' and their lives would be saved. Now, what should I have done under these circumstances? And I speak not simply personally, but in a representative capacity, for I think the rest of you are very much like myself. With my head on the block I suspect I should have said, 'Hold on! I think I can make a statement that will be satisfactory to all sides.' " For too long, Christians have been like that, accommodating, worldly-wise, pliable, acquiescing in what is conventional, leaving their unbelieving neighbours uncertain as to what the Church stands for, unless it is an easy-going toleration of things as they are, coupled with a mild desire that they may grow better in time, so far as that is compatible with the maintenance of vested interests. Salt, light, leaven—those were the terms Jesus used in envisaging the impact of his disciples on the world. And to-day, the greatest danger confronting the Church is not that it will die. The Church will not die. The ever-present danger which confronts the Church is that it may become insipid—standing for nothing in particular, hesitant, half-hearted, its message muffled and uncertain.

How is that to be prevented? How in point of fact has it been prevented? When has the Church been like salt and light and leaven, its influence potent, its temper militant? Not alone when its members have had robust convictions and an overpowering sense of divine election but when they have been *in close, intimate daily touch with Christ, their Saviour and Master.* "I know whom I have believed," cried Paul. Not what but whom. Ideas have legs but men, if they are to be stirred to action, must have more than ideas. Ideas, like ideals, are poor ghosts until they become incarnate. Back of the idea is the person animating it. Back of the movement is the leader directing and inspiring it—Buddha, Mahomet, Napoleon, Lenin, Hitler, Gandhi, Christ. Certainly Christ had no compunction in attaching men to himself. He taught them to yield their faith to him, and in generation after generation that is what thousands upon thousands have done. He has become the object of their faith, their Law, their Light their Leader, their Lord. It is he who has inspired their sense of conviction. It is from him they have caught the sense of vocation. Under the constraint born of association with him they have gone forth as on a great venture to labour for the Kingdom of God. He has given them, to quote David Christie, a world they can live in, a cause they can live for, a self they can live with, a Master they can die for. They have brought life to the Church and help and healing to the world.

Where in such matters as these do we stand? The question is a personal one and must be personally answered. One thing I know. If to-day you and I make a fresh, or a first, dedication of our lives to Christ, resolve to serve his cause with the same ardour and intensity of devotion that others give to the service of causes far less worthy and deserving, the winds of God will blow through this church and we shall see His mighty acts done in our midst and far beyond it.

Can We Follow Jesus To-day?

CHRISTIANITY began not with subscription to a creed but with attachment to a person. Jesus initiated a movement that is now world-wide by going out and individually enlisting disciples. "Follow me" was what he said to Andrew and Simon, James and John and Matthew, and scores of others. He had no scruples in asking men for unreserved loyalty to himself. He had no hesitation in presenting himself to them as their Leader and Exemplar. He told them that they must be prepared to give up everything, to give it up at once, to rise without a word whether of excuse or protest and go after him. "Follow me" was the sum of all that he had to say to men.

Nineteen hundred years have passed and men are still being urged to follow Jesus. But how is it to be done? Can it be done? Those are not captious questions. The people who raise them are people whose interest is neither casual nor superficial. They recognize the nobility of the teaching of Jesus and acknowledge its originality and distinctiveness. More than that, in a general way they approve it and say that they would like to be able to conform to it and to see others, nations as well as individuals, do the same. But they have their difficulties.

One of them is the difficulty of relating Jesus to the concrete situations in which they find themselves today. How is a twentieth-century American to walk in the steps of a life that was lived in the first century and in such markedly different circumstances? Here we are in a highly complex, mechanized, industrialized and competitive society, whereas Jesus lived in a society largely rural and pastoral. It is not only the setting but the character of the life that is different. He neither married nor set up a home. He left the carpenter's shop to become an itinerant preacher. His attitude to the government of his time was more detached than would be warranted in conscientious citizens to-day. The simplicity of his life and the excellence of his character make an unfailing appeal. But with family claims, business interests, property concerns and civic obligations pressing upon them, what men who get down to thinking about the matter of taking Jesus seriously want to know is whether it is possible for them to transfer any pattern of behaviour from his life to their own.

The crux of the difficulty is this: Is the teaching of Jesus relevant to contemporary life? Does it afford the detailed and specific direction people need as they grapple with the moral dilemmas which beset them amid the complexity of the modern world? Some of the best minds of our generation profess to be disappointed by what seem to them the limitations and inadequacies of Jesus' teaching in this respect. So many of their problems, they say, are not as much as mentioned in the Gospels, especially the problems of public life—the possession of property, the nature of government, the policies of nations in their dealings with one another.

But this is to misunderstand what Jesus came to do. It is to turn to his teaching in the expectation of finding there a set of rules, a code, an ethical guide-book covering every contingency in life and providing rule of thumb directions for all ethical dilemmas, personal and social. There is no such code in the Gospels.

Jesus was in no sense a legislator. He made no attempt, for his own day any more than for ours, at supplying a complete compendium of moral duties. What he did was to describe a way of life and exhibit it in action. By word and deed he set forth spiritual attitudes, moral principles which are timeless and universal in their validity and as relevant in our industrialized age as in agricultural Palestine, principles like "Love your enemies" and "Whatsoever ye would that men should do to you, do you even so to them."

Jesus was a prophet, not a legislator. Had he legislated his teaching would inevitably have been outmoded with the passage of the years. A code which prescribes how men are to behave, irrespective of changing needs and changing conditions, even though it claims to be final, is out of the running from the start. The Koran claims to be final but as an ethical directory—and no one is more keenly aware of this than the liberal Moslem—it is a moral and social anachronism. Jesus by comparison left no law-book, no code governing behaviour at every turn of the road of life. He put men into touch with great creative principles and faced each individual and each generation with the task—the admittedly difficult task—of working out their implications and applying them in specific contemporary situations. The value of his teaching is not in telling us how we ought to behave in every circumstance and in every relationship but in describing a way of life to be worked out in personal character and social relationships.

So long as this is remembered no one is likely to label Jesus' teaching antiquated or irrelevant. Too much can be made of the difference between his world and ours. In many ways it was a world strikingly like our own. Then as now there were people organizing their grievances in self-righteous pressure groups—insisting on their rights, aggressive, grasping. Then as now the Haves were ranged against the Have-nots and there was suspicion and animosity and friction. Then as now there were wars and rumours of wars, and back of them exploitation, oppression and unrest. Christ lived in a world which in essentials was extraordinarily like our own.

Moreover, the truths he taught, the issues he dealt with are timeless, as old and new at once as nature's self. He addressed himself to that in the human heart which does not change with the years—its loves and hates, its hopes and fears, its joys and sorrows, its temptations and passions and failures. He spoke of sin, the bitterest of all human troubles, and how deliverance from it can be found. He spoke of the cares and anxieties of daily existence and pointed the way to a simple, unharassed life. He spoke of the human soul, of its worth, its rights, its possibilities, its responsibilities. He spoke confidently and convincingly of God as the Father of men, answering and satisfying the deepest craving of their spirits. What is there in this that is irrelevant to-day? What is there that would justify us in imprisoning Jesus in the fetters of the first century and denying his validity now? I recall something George Matheson once wrote: "Son of Man, whenever I doubt of life, I think of Thee. Nothing is so impossible as that Thou shouldest be dead . . . Thou never growest old to me. Last century is old, last year is an obsolete fashion, but Thou art not obsolete. Thou art abreast of all the centuries. I have never come up with Thee, modern as I am."

Poetic rhapsodizing, does some one say? No, for what Matheson claimed is historical fact. Jesus never has been imprisoned within the fetters of a particular age and environment. It is the rarest thing to see a man step out intellectually ahead of his time, but Jesus is not only ahead of his time, he towers above every generation. You cannot date Jesus. He spans all the centuries. "Heaven and earth," he calmly said, "shall pass away, but my words shall not pass away." In point of actual fact his words are as alive with spiritual appeal in the twentieth century as in the first; they are

the living contemporaries of every age. Can you conceive of a
generation for whom the Beatitudes or the parable of the good
Samaritan or the Golden Rule would not be profoundly relevant
and to whom they would carry no spiritual challenge or conviction? Christianity has been carried to every nation in the
world, and is unfolding to each generation the true interpretation
of that generation's life because its Founder was untrammelled by
any provincialisms, and the truths he taught were universal and
eternal. Even a thinker like Renan acknowledged as much. "Whatever the surprises of history," he said, "Jesus will never be sur-
passed."

There is, however, another and greater difficulty. For some, it
is not the irrelevance of Jesus to contemporary life that is the
problem. They see that he speaks to our situation, diagnoses our
sickness, offers as a solution of our predicament a new way of
life. What they doubt is the practicability of the solution. The
way of life is beautiful and noble but is it not far too idealistic,
too high and too hard for ordinary people? At times they feel
inclined to attempt it, but they are deterred by the fear that it
will be impossible for them to keep it up, that they will not be able
to rise to it, and so they persuade themselves that they must have
something easier, something not so demanding or perfectionist,
and that the honest thing is to make no pretence of being a
Christian.

Of all attitudes to Jesus this is the commonest. It is the real
attitude of thousands who attend church and have their names
on its membership lists. The idea of applying the principles of
Jesus either to their business or to their politics does not seem to
them practicable. One often hears it said that there would soon be
an end of all our troubles if only people would act in accordance
with the teaching of Jesus. It is a big "if." The thing is easier said
than done. It is not half so simple as the people who repeat such

platitudes seem to think. It would be a wonderful world if everybody lived by the principles of the Sermon on the Mount, but with those principles so demanding, with the world what it is and human nature what it is, what prospect is there of such a world?

It is wholesome to raise that question. It is wholesome to face up to the uncommonly high standards which Jesus sets us. Let me name some of them. We are to put God and not self first. We are not to be anxious about food or clothes or money. We are to be absolutely honest. We are to love our enemies and forgive until seventy times seven. We are to be perfect as God is perfect. What honouring claims Jesus made on human nature! What an optimist he was! Men did not always show him their best side but he believed in them and in their ability to rise to the height of his challenge. He never despaired of humanity. He was always calling on men to be bigger and braver and wiser and more Godlike in the living of their lives. He never spoke as though evil were permanently rooted in the order of things or as though the meaner elements in human nature were ineradicable. It was because he saw men as children of God that he made such exacting demands and pitched things so high.

We need a faith like that to-day. There are too many among us taking a dim view of man, decrying and belittling him, repeating the old cliché that human nature is human nature and that there is nothing we can do about it. If there is poverty in the world that's because men are naturally improvident. If there is unemployment that's because they are naturally lazy. If there are wars that's because men are naturally belligerent. If men cheat and outsmart one another in cut-throat competition that's because they are naturally selfish. On this view the mean and debasing elements in humanity are incorrigible and ineradicable. To talk about the Golden Rule and the brotherhood of man and a warless world is a waste of breath.

Of all the obstacles standing in the way of a better world this is the most powerful. Anybody who has worked for the betterment of his fellows knows that the biggest difficulty he has to contend with is cynicism about the possibility of changing human nature. It is cynicism that leads men to say about greed and graft and slums and prostitution and war, "These are things that always have been and always will be." There was no such cynicism in Jesus. He was not blind to the evil in man but there was something else he never lost sight of—the wonderful latent goodness in ordinary men and women. He saw hidden possibilities in everybody he met and believed that they could be called into life. His standards are high, but he did not expect men to rise to them unaided. He told them that power was available whereby they could not only rise to them but keep them.

It is this that nine persons out of ten forget. They look at the standards of Jesus and feel instinctively that it is beyond their power to keep them. They fail to realize that they are not asked to keep them in their own strength. What a wealth of suggestion James Hilton put into the title of one of his novels—*We Are Not Alone*. It is what the New Testament keeps saying to us. We are not left to ourselves. None of us is obliged to rely only on his own resources. God is always at hand to enable the person who will turn to Him to do things which are impossible to mere human nature. Jesus repeatedly emphasized that—that if we would get into touch with God we would find ourselves able to rise on stepping-stones of our dead selves to finer and better things. His promise, "Ye shall receive power," is as fundamental a part of his message as his watchword, "Seek ye first the kingdom of God."

I say again, nine persons out of ten forget that. They go back to the historical Jesus for a way of life to be worked out in personal relationships, and they stop there. If that way of life is to become a reality for them they will have to learn to live by the help and grace of God. There was Jesus' secret. He lived by the help and grace of God. Day by day, hour by hour, he drew on Divine resources. And he taught that all of us, day by day, hour by hour, may do the same.

We are here at the heart of the whole matter. To follow Jesus is not easy. The gate is strait and the way narrow. But if we have the desire to follow him, and will turn daily to God for strength, a power will take possession of us that will enable us to dare and do the impossible. This is not romancing. It has happened in generation after generation. It is the experience of men and women here. I must be speaking to some who are drawn to Christ's way of life, who are sure that if there is to be any salvation for the world it will have to be along the line of Jesus, but who fear that his standards are beyond their reach. Will you remember that you are not alone? You can draw on Divine resources. Power is available to live victoriously. Christ's way is hard and high but recall what he said when his disciples thought it so hard and high that nobody could rise to it—"With men it is impossible, but with God all things are possible."

Can Human Nature Be Changed?

D ICK SHEPPARD used to tell a story about a man who sat drinking in a bar. He had been drinking for a long time. He had swallowed considerable quantities of liquor. And as he drank, he wept. He wept because he had wasted his life. He wept because he had failed to do his duty by his family. He wept because he had never appreciated his wife properly. He wept because somehow his good intentions always went wrong. But never mind, he told himself, this time it would be different. He would redeem the past and make up for everything. All, he resolved, would yet be well. He felt uplifted and noble at the very thought. His mind glowed with a genial assurance of virtue. Just then the bartender said, "Time, gentlemen, please"—*and he went home and swore at his wife.*

Can anything be done for a man like that, a man whose intentions are honourable but whose performances are lamentable? He wants to be a better man, but what do his wishes amount to? He is to-day substantially what he was a year ago; he has the same old and apparently inveterate faults and failings. Indeed, the chances are that instead of improving he has grown worse, is weaker in will and grosser in desire. Is there anything that can bring about a change in him and so transform his whole nature as to make him what, in his best moments, he fain would be?

Some people are emphatically of the opinion that nothing can be done. Any chance of reforming an individual beyond the period of adolescence is simply hopeless. By then the faults of temper and temperament are too deeply embedded in the character to be rooted out and destroyed. They are as much a part of the individual as his skin. He may spruce himself up a bit, apply a little polish here, work down an excrescence there, but the main outline and quality of his character—nothing can alter that.

A newspaper columnist, whose views are read by hundreds of thousands and whose name is a household word, recently, and in forthright fashion, expressed the point thus: "If a man is a philanderer, he will be a philanderer to the end. It is only in novels that a miracle occurs in the last chapter that makes the drunkard reform and become sober, the grouch sunny and sweet-tempered, the miser generous and open-handed, the shrew so mild that butter wouldn't melt in her mouth. In real life these things never happen. People continue to be what habit and usage have made them."

There is nothing vague or ambiguous about that view-point, but if it is clear-cut and dogmatic, it is also dreadfully dismal and pessimistic, and one wonders whether those who propound it or who subscribe to it have really thought out in terms of strict logic its implications and consequences. We are all weary and sick of the world we know, a world of fear and hate and greed and slaughter. We are all longing and hoping for a new world, a world that will guarantee justice and security, quietness and peace. But with the passing of every day it becomes increasingly evident that we shall never have and never preserve a new world unless and until fear and hate and greed and pride are purged from human hearts. According to the view just described, such a purge is impossible. Human nature cannot be changed. Nothing can be done for a person if years of habit, or of environment, or of heredity, have bent his character into one shape, and that shape is crooked or deformed. The drunkard will always be a drunkard. The sensualist will always be a sensualist. The world will always be at the mercy of crooks and gangsters and upstart dictators.

It is a dreadfully dismal and pessimistic conclusion to be driven to, and it is made so much the more so when one thinks not—as we have been doing up to this point—of single individuals but of humanity at large. For consider what such a conclusion involves. There is no abiding or ultimate cure for the ills of humanity. Nothing can be done permanently to heal its hurt. In human nature there is an incorrigible element which means that history is bound to go on repeating itself to the end. Because of the terrible things that have been happening in the world since the opening of the century, because of the disappointed hopes and the disillusionment that have followed in the wake of two world wars, people in all ranks of life are capitulating, or are under heavy pressure to capitulate, to depression and despair. I quote from a notable speech made by Mr. Winston Churchill in the autumn of 1946: "Certainly the scene we survey bears many uncomfortable resemblances to that of 1938. Indeed, in some respects, it is even darker. The peoples of Europe have fallen immeasurably deeper into the pit of misery and confusion. Many of their cities are in ruins. Millions of their homes have been destroyed. They have torn one another into pieces with more ferocity, on a larger scale, and with more deadly weapons than ever before. But have they found stable and lasting peace? Is the brotherhood of mankind any nearer? Has the reign of law returned? Alas, although the resources and vitality of nearly all the European countries are woefully diminished, many of their old hatreds burn on with undying flame. Skeletons with gleaming eyes . . . glare at each other across the ashes and rubble heap of what was once the august Roman Empire and later a Christian civilization. Is there never to be an end? Is there no salvation here below? Are we to sink through gradations of infinite suffering to primordial levels—

> A discord. Dragons of the prime,
> That tear each other in their slime

or can we avoid our doom?"

Can we avoid our doom? Can human nature be changed? Can man's ethical capacity catch up with his scientific skill? In one form or another, that is the question of the hour. Statesmen are asking it. Scientists are asking it. Philosophers and educationists and churchmen are asking it. And the man on the street, as he reads his newspaper and listens to the radio and talks with his friends, is asking it too. Is there a way out of the muddle we are in? Is there any salvation here below? Is evil so endemic in human nature as to be incurable, or is there a remedy, a sovereign remedy for it?

Did I say that is the question of the hour? It is the question of the ages. There is nothing new about such a question. In century after century men have asked it. But there is this to bear in mind. Deep down in the human heart there is something that refuses to take "No" as the answer. The pessimists and cynics, like the poor, are always with us, and they and their positions have to be reckoned with and not ignored, but they are never really in the majority. "Hope springs eternal in the human breast." "Man," as Nietzsche said, "is a recurring decimal." You can never work him out. You may divide and divide to your heart's content, but each figure you get, so far from being the end is simply a new beginning. There is something invincible and indestructible in man. The visions he cherishes may become dim but they do not die. The torch is handed on from generation to generation. Even when the night is at its darkest the song may be heard—

> These things shall be,—a loftier race
> Than ere the world hath known shall
>   rise
> With flame of freedom in their souls,
> And light of knowledge in their eyes.

Mark that last line—"And light of knowledge in their eyes." It offers a clue to the hopes of so many. If they refuse to despair of human nature or of the possibility of achieving a new and better order, it is because of what they believe knowledge can do, provided only that it is given a chance and on a big enough scale—the ignorance it can dispel, the prejudice it can overcome, the miraculous transformation it can work both in the broadening and elevating of men's minds and in the refining and enriching of their characters. That is the case for education as one of the cures —there are those who think it is the major cure—for the ills of humanity. Presented at its best, it is a strong case. It is being advocated with passionate faith and conviction by men and women who see civilization engaged in a race with catastrophe and who are desperate to avert a crash. There are some things one notices about that advocacy. One is the growing tendency to acknowledge and deplore the diminution of spiritual values in the contemporary world bound up with training of a purely vocational character. As a scientist remarked not long ago, if education is wholly given over to specialization on vocationally useful pursuits it will tend to produce young barbarians who know nothing of the rich heritage of culture and are blind outside their own narrow field. Another is the anxiety that the knowledge made available by education should be turned to constructive rather than destructive ends; that atomic energy should be used not to blast the world but to rebuild it; and as with the new physics, so with the new biology, the new chemistry, the new engineering—that instead of producing poisons capable of blotting out cities, and infections of such violence and virulence as to wipe out whole communities, and bombs destructive enough to reduce to a hideous rubble the fruits of human labour for a thousand years, the awesome power within our reach and at our command should be employed to raise the standard of living of all the peoples, to bring peace, plenty and tranquility.

There is another thing one notices. It is the recognition on the part of many educationists that something more than education is needed if human nature is to be changed and a new and better order established. Witness the judgement of Sir Richard Livingstone, the President of Corpus Christi College, Oxford: "We and our education have been too absorbed in the matter of life to think of its spirit. We must restore to it a vitamin, deficient both there and in our life—a religion, a philosophy of living, a definite ideal to guide, discipline and dominate the lives of individuals and, through them, national life."

It is an impressive judgement. Not all are disposed to approve it. Many prefer to make legislation the ally of education. Isn't that the significance of the experiment being carried out in Soviet Russia? And Soviet Russia apart, legislation has on its credit side a long list of remarkable achievements. My background being British, I think at once of the Repeal of the Corn Laws under Cobden, of the introduction of the Factory Acts associated with the name of Lord Shaftesbury, of the emancipation of the slaves in the West Indies and of Wilberforce's labours to make it effective by statute. I have no doubt that you, for your part, are thinking of events no less striking in America's story. Nor need attention be confined to the past. No one can deny that wise, impartial, far-sighted legislation is needed now if catastrophe is to be averted; it is needed on a world-wide scale. And in the case of the United Nations it is being set up—slowly, laboriously, painfully under our very eyes here in New York City. We are the witnesses of an attempt which has for its goal nothing less than a radical, thoroughgoing change in human nature, and which merits the constant and vigilant support of men and women of good will everywhere.

And yet our real problem lies deeper—deeper than either education or legislation. There is a passage in Trotsky's *Literature and Revolution* which makes pathetic reading, especially in view of Trotsky's end. He is writing about the change of spirit to become manifest with the establishment of the Communist Revolution. "All the emotions which we revolutionists at the present time feel apprehensive of naming—so much have they been worn thin by hypocrites—such as disinterested friendship, love for one's neighbours, sympathy—will be the mighty ringing words of socialist poetry. . . . All will be equally interested in the success of the whole. There will be no running after profits. There will be nothing mean, no betrayals, no bribery, none of the things which form the soul of competition in a society divided into classes." What ruined that Utopia? One thing—unregenerate human nature. We have got to get behind the system to the men who comprise it. No legal framework, no external organization of society, no school or college curriculum will of itself transform character or guarantee that people who before were competitive and grasping and unprincipled over night become the opposite. Behind the problem of a warless world lies the prior problem of the people who are to live in it as brothers. As Herbert Spencer put it: "There is no political alchemy by which you can get golden conduct out of leaden instincts."

Is there any alchemy by which you can get golden conduct out of leaden instincts? Yes, there is. Alongside of education and legislation there can be set another term—Regeneration. If Christianity affirms anything at all, it affirms that human nature can be changed, genuinely, radically and permanently changed. The drunkard can reform and become sober, the impure can become pure, the grouch can become genial, the individual who is plagued with temper or temperament can be helped to integrate his personality and can learn the secret of self-control, the crook and the gangster, yes, and the upstart dictator can be won to a new frame of mind and to a new way of life.

No one who appreciates the issues that are at stake here will be disposed either to ignore or to treat lightly this claim. If it is false,

its falsity should be exposed. If it is true, the truth should be pro-
claimed as with the sound of a trumpet. It is not too much to say
that Christianity stands or falls by its claim to transform human
nature. As one writer expressed it, deliberately putting the thought
into the most provocative form of words he could devise, "If Jesus
Christ cannot make character, he can make nothing else." But he
can make character. He has been making it for sixty generations.
He found the nature of Zacchaeus greedy and he changed it. He
found the nature of Augustine lustful and he changed it. He found
the nature of Elizabeth Fry indolent and he changed it.

The evidence is from the present as well as the past. One of the
glories of the Christian religion is that every day it raises up new
witnesses; it produces fresh evidence of its validity and virility
as it goes along. Take, for instance, the testimony of Hugh Red-
wood, a prominent member of the staff of the London *Daily News:*
"If you should ask me by what authority I talk about the power
of Christ to change human nature, I should reply to you simply
(and God knows without one word or thought of boasting) because he has changed my nature. I can look anybody in the face
to-day—my friends, my colleagues, and what, perhaps, is most
difficult of all, the members of my own household and family—
and be sure that they know, as I know, that I am really and literally
a new creature in Christ Jesus since the day when he came into my
life."

What do we make of that? And it is only one instance. There
are so many others, all of them unanswerable arguments for Christianity. Unless for nineteen hundred years people have been com-
bining in a vast conspiracy to talk claptrap and humbug, Christ
can change and renew human nature, can solve the moral problems
of existence. And the moral problems, not the political or the
economic ones, are the prior and basic problems of existence.
People like you and me have had their natures changed by Christ.

Drunkards have become sober, misers have become generous and open-handed, tempery individuals who have made themselves and other people miserable by their tantrums have found the way to self-control. Not only in novels, but in real life these things have happened. By the grace of God and the power of Christ people have ceased to be any longer what usage and habit had made them.

What about us? Does our nature need changing? And have we found, when we have tried to change it, that we are unable to get at the seat of the trouble? The fact is that no one working single-handed and alone can change himself. To attempt self-reform without Divine grace is to be like Sisyphus, rolling a stone uphill only to find it come down again with greater force. It is to have a bow without a sling, a sword without a blade. Henry Ward Beecher in his autobiography describes the never-to-be-forgotten morning when—to quote his own words—"I found out that it is God's nature to love man in his sin for the purpose of helping him out of it, as my mother loved me when I was in trouble that she might help me out of it. Then," he says, "I found God." That goes to the heart of the matter. The secret of a changed nature lies there.

Why Not Do What Comes Naturally?

I T IS probably unnecessary to acknowledge that the title of the
sermon for to-day is borrowed. I have taken it from a song in
a musical comedy which ran on Broadway for many months. That
a preacher should go for the subject of his sermon to such a source
may seem strange, and in the case of such a song, indefensible as
well as strange. When a man has a book like the Bible for a source
book why, unless he is a sensation monger or mentally bankrupt,
should he turn to Broadway for ideas?

The question is a fair one. Let me give you the answer. Here
is a song by a popular composer. From the day of its production
it has been what we call a hit. Through the medium of the theatre, of the radio, and of recordings the words and music have
become known to hundreds of thousands. The words are not in-
nocuous. It will not do to say that they are amusing or diverting
or vulgar or suggestive, but no more than that. There is behind
them a philosophy of life which is being accepted uncritically
by more people, especially adolescents, than one likes to think
of, a philosophy of life which is at loggerheads with Christian
standards and ideals and involves their negation.

What is that philosophy? It is that we all have appetites, impulses, urges which are native to us. They do not have to be

acquired; they do not have to be learned; they are instinctive. Since they are that, since they are natural why should we not follow them? In point of fact, Christian standards and ideals notwithstanding, it is what people, old and young, simple and sophisticated, do.

Compressed into a few sentences, that is the philosophy of the song. It has been elaborated in recent years in many a book. Men and women have been exhorted to "follow nature," to insist upon their right to free self-expression, to experience, to happiness, and there has been no end of scornful comment regarding old-fashioned restraints and conventions. It is comfortable doctrine. It excuses us from any attempt at self-control. We are all made with a strong inclination toward self-indulgence and with an equally strong inclination away from self-discipline. There is no rebutting the assertion of C. S. Lewis that chastity is the most unpopular of the Christian virtues. The very name of moralist has become, as Walter Lippmann points out, a term of disparagement and suggests a somewhat pretentious and a somewhat stupid, perhaps even a somewhat hypocritical meddler in other people's lives.

Notice, however, what happens again and again when this philosophy is adopted and put into practice. Liberty degenerates into licence. Following nature is taken to mean: Gratify your desires, obey your impulses, express yourself freely. It results in the capitulation of reason and will to feeling and exalts what is primitive and merely animal to a primacy to which it has no claim. It turns out people who are governed by their senses and who consider that the existence of desire is all the justification that is needed for its gratification. There is a constant tendency, apparent in one contemporary novel after another, for naturalism to degenerate into animalism.

Think of the life which so many live to-day—a life of coarse pleasures and excitements. "Let yourself go," they say. "Have a good time. Don't be handicapped by your inhibitions. Indulge every whim and passion—and damn the consequences." They may be ready light-heartedly enough to damn the consequences, but they had better be careful that the consequences do not damn them. They are having a good time but how long will it last? First they will experience boredom and ennui, for self-indulgence works strictly according to the law of diminishing returns. Then they will crave bigger and still bigger doses of artificial stimulant to quieten the mind, drug the senses and muffle the conscience. And finally there will come exhaustion and confusion, failure of nerve and total collapse, which is the price that must always be paid sooner or later for moral anarchy.

I draw attention to this because there is an impression abroad that modern psychology supports the contention that in order to avoid unhealthy complexes we should follow our nature and give expression to our appetites and instincts. Nearly everybody has heard of the dangers and evil consequences of repression, and some conclude, not unwillingly, from what they have heard that they should give their appetites and instincts free rein. Yet it would be difficult to find an argument in the work of any reputable and judicious psychologist or psychoanalyst, including Sigmund Freud, which countenances such a deduction. Repression, it should be remembered, is a technical term. It is not the same thing as self-control. To get at its meaning we should set alongside of it in our minds the word "suppression."

Suppression is the deliberate refusal to translate into action the impulses to undesirable courses of conduct. It is conscious and voluntary control, the calculated subjugation of such instinctive energies as we cannot use in their biological way. It is what the Bible means by temperance; it is self-discipline; it is the quality in a man which enables him to hold himself in check and say "No" to the mob of his appetites and desires. Browning who was sure that it strengthened moral fibre wrote:

> Why comes temptation, but for
>   man to meet
> And master, and make crouch
>   beneath his feet,
> And so be pedestaled in triumph?

This sort of moral athleticism never did anybody any harm. It is wholesome and healthy. It is an absolutely essential element in the fight for character. By means of it men have risen above the flux of the merely instinctive life, have become masters of themselves and thereby masters of their world. So much is this the case that one finds a psychologist like McDougall insisting that suppression *is* civilization. "Without it, without restraint, without self-control, without deliberate choice between good and evil, between the greater and the lesser good, without laws and without conventions, there can be nothing but chaos and savagery in the worst sense, there can be none of the finer things of life."

Now and by contrast observe what repression is. I have been emphasizing that suppression is wholesome and healthy. To a man the psychologists are unanimous in affirming that repression is harmful and dangerous. We should be careful to observe why. Suppression acknowledges the existence of instincts and appetites and sets itself to keep them disciplined and in order. Repression refuses to acknowledge them, seeks to keep them out of the conscious region of the mind, usually because it is shocked or frightened by them, or because it is ashamed of them, or because they are illegitimate, and it finishes up by driving them underground. I imagine that we all know people who repress in this harmful sense. They disguise from themselves the true nature of their impulses. They pretend to themselves that they are not angry;

they refuse to recognize that they are jealous, or envious, or covetous, or sensuous when those tendencies are really at work in them. They are strangers to self-criticism and self-control.

But to refuse to acknowledge the existence of an impulse and thereby to drive it down into the subconscious is to invite trouble. For the subconscious is not a grave but a laboratory; it is not a storehouse but a mill. Forced into the cellar of the mind the instincts do not cease to exist; they are not idle or inactive; they are potential dynamite and as such liable to produce an explosion; they strive continually to return to consciousness and use up a great deal of nervous energy in the effort. There is so much maladjusted emotion adhering to them that they can work havoc both on the body and the mind and threaten the integrity of the entire personality. It is only in proportion as we recognize and accept our instincts that we can control and sublimate them.

"Never repress" is sound advice but we should make sure that we understand what it means. What the psychologist understands by it is that in the interests of the moral life and of a sound mind we must fully and frankly acknowledge the existence in us of impulses and instincts like those of fear and of sex. "Never repress" does *not* mean "never suppress." It is not an invitation to licence, to a life uninhibited and undisciplined. There is no sanction in psychology for the view that full rein should be given to all those instinctive energies which are at work in human nature. Nor is there any in ethical religion. If this view is right, then the old moralists, like Plato, and more recent moralists, like Kant, and all Christian moralists are wrong. Something that Spinoza once said belongs here, "To those who want salvation cheap, and most men do, there is very little comfort to be had out of the great teachers." One and all they insist that the good life is attainable only through the stern subordination of appetite and instinct. And none more than Christ with his ultimatum,

"If any man will come after me, let him deny himself and take up his cross and follow me." Is there anybody here who maintains that the existence of desire is all the justification that is needed for its gratification? What do you make of that ultimatum? What, moreover, do you suppose Christ meant when he declared, "If thy hand offend thee, cut it off; if thine eye offend thee, pluck it out; it is better for thee to enter into life maimed, than to have a whole body given up to the consuming fire"?

The philosophy which says, "Gratify your desires, obey your impulses, let yourself go," is a comfortable philosophy, and for that reason it will always be a popular one. Nevertheless, anyone who proposes to defend it should realize that he is taking on a formidable assignment. Is there a great name in any century that can be quoted in its support? On the other hand, the arguments that can be marshalled against it are difficult to refute.

Naturalism is a terribly narrow philosophy. It decides everything by reference to feeling and makes man a creature of impulse. It forgets that the feeling part of human nature is the uncritical part of it. Once passion is roused it is apt to be a law to itself and to seek no sanction outside of itself. To give in to passion, however, to refuse to subordinate it to reason or to hold it in check by strength of will, is to behave not like a man but like an animal. The person who has never learned to say "No" to his appetites, whose mind is used to gratify his desires, not to discipline them or to bring them into harmony with his ideals, is far from comprehending the nature of human life as contrasted with animal existence.

Naturalism is also a terribly selfish philosophy. It is selfish because, as a moment's reflection will demonstrate, you cannot take an exhortation like "Gratify your desires, obey your impulses, let yourself go," and generalize it. You may claim self-gratification as a right for yourself but you are bound to hesitate before permitting it to all and sundry. Think what would happen if all men were to follow their nature, if everybody did what was right in his own eyes, indulged every whim and passion, let himself go. Chaos and misery would be the result. The reason why some people are able to indulge themselves and their appetites is because they are members of a society which is held together by men and women with a different and nobler philosophy of life. Let us not mince words about such people. They are parasites. The measure of their selfishness is that they treat their fellows not as persons but as things, not as ends but as means to an end. "Love your neighbour as yourself," says Jesus. It is impossible to love your neighbour as yourself if you make a tool of him or if he—or she—serves merely to gratify your desires.

Compare with the philosophy I have been describing the Christian philosophy. It is grounded on the conviction that the body is the temple of the Holy Spirit. Paul, whose phrase that is, regarded the body as sacred, as the dwelling-place of the divine, as the human vehicle or medium for the thought and action of God. "Glorify God in your body," he tells the Corinthians. To the Philippians he says, "Christ shall be magnified in my body." To the Romans his injunction is, "I beseech you therefore, brethren, by the mercies of God, that you present your bodies a living sacrifice, holy, acceptable unto God, which is your reasonable service." It is on this ground that he bases the obligation to chastity. Sensuality is sacrilege. Sexual transgression defiles the soul and drives the Holy Spirit out of it. The supreme motive for continence is neither consideration of the wrong done to another, grievous as that is, nor the ascetic motive of crushing the lower appetites, necessary as that is, but the obligation, binding and absolute, to keep the body as well as the soul free from sin. "Shall I take the members of Christ and make them the members of a prostitute?" is Paul's most characteristic inquiry. It is just as pointed and just as relevant to-day as it was in the first century.

But if in one breath Paul tells the Corinthians that the body is the temple of the Holy Spirit in the next he goes on to add, "I maul and master my body, in case, after preaching to other people, I am disqualified myself." Is Paul contradicting himself? Is he saying in one sentence that the body is sacred and in the next that it is evil? No! What he is emphasizing is that he spares no pains to get the mastery over it. The body is not evil but it is the avenue by which temptation makes its approach to the soul. The body is not evil but it has to be subordinated to the soul. It is not the senior partner in the house of life. The almost universal tendency is to forget that, and forgetting it, to indulge the body, to permit it to be the master when it should be the servant, to neglect the higher for the lower, to pamper the one and starve the other, so that the flesh in the end suffocates the spirit. The process may be seen going on every day—men and women becoming heavy, dull and slow, their will weak, their temper moody, their spiritual affections languid.

It was this that Paul schooled himself to avoid. He was no ascetic. He knew that pride may be pampered while the flesh grows lean. He honoured the body as the temple of the Spirit of God but he felt that he was honouring it most when he strove to make it the dutiful and submissive servant of the soul. He was no ascetic but he was a spiritual athlete. He strove for the mastery in a field where most people are hard put to it to pass muster. He did not pamper or surfeit or pollute his body lest by doing so he should stupify or drug his soul.

Not self-indulgence but self-discipline is the Christian rule. Did I say the Christian rule? If one wants to be or become something in any field of life it is the universal rule. The artist, the author, the musician, the scientist, the tight-rope walker can only achieve success by innumerable renunciations, by an immense concentration, by killing out the smaller centres of interest. There can be no frittering of energy, no mixture of motives. "Every poem," Francis Thompson said, "is a human sacrifice." One of Ruskin's pupils told him, "The instant I entered the gallery at Florence I knew what you meant by the supremacy of Botticelli." "In an instant did you?" said Ruskin; "it took me twenty years to find out." Ask any master of his craft for his secret—Einstein, Paderewski, Fosdick. You always get the same answer—Genius is an infinite capacity for taking pains. And you never have an infinite capacity for taking pains without self-discipline.

With religion, too, it is like that. We began with ANNIE GET YOUR GUN. We conclude on a different note. Listen! "Blessed are the pure in heart; for they shall see God." "If any man will do His will, he shall know of the doctrine." "Enter ye in at the strait gate . . . because strait is the gate, and narrow is the way, that leadeth unto life; and few there be that find it." "Do you not know that in a race, though all run, only one man gains the prize? Run so as to win the prize. Every athlete practices self-restraint all round; but while they do it to win a fading wreath, we do it for an unfading. Well, I run without swerving; I do not plant my blows upon the empty air—no, I maul and master my body, in case, after preaching to other people, I am disqualified myself."

What To Do With Our Fears?

THESE are days when fear is in the very air we breathe. Has there ever been a generation as frightened as ours? Not long ago, reading at random, I came upon a passage which, in the light of current events, makes for melancholy reflection. It was in a book written in 1902 by George Coe and this, with special reference to the achievements of science, is what he was affirming: "Men have ceased to be afraid. We have our own unsolved problems, as our fathers did, but they awaken little mystic presentiment, and no fear. We do not catch our breath at the thought of what may be, but boldly take to pieces every new phenomenon, certain in advance that it harbors no hobgoblins." The atomic bomb has put an end to all such sentiments. Two world wars in twenty-five years, with a third on the near horizon, have awakened the profoundest misgiving and apprehension. Everywhere there are people who are fretful, nervous, depressed, irritable, sleepless, physically under par, and the basic reason is because they are the victims of fear. Who was it said that the first thing from which we have to be saved is fear?

This is an area of human experience which involves us all, young and old, rich and poor, wise and simple. The range of fear, the variety of the forms it assumes, is astonishing. Psychologists say that we come into the world with only two inborn fears—the fear of falling and the fear of loud noises—and that all the others are acquired or induced. There is no denying that as we grow older our fears multiply. If I were to try to enumerate them the list would be a long one—fear of losing work, of illness, of responsibility, of failure, of being left on the shelf, of growing old, of bereavement and death; fear not only for ourselves but for others—our loved ones and what the chances and changes of life may do to them; fear for our country, for the good estate of the world, for the future of civilization. Worst of all is the boding, shapeless, nameless dread which has no definite source or cause but which by its intensity can sap our energy and vitality, leaving us helpless and hopeless.

Some of our fears are fantastic. We have all laughed over the lion tamer who could overawe the fiercest of wild animals with a glance yet went in terror of the little slip of a woman who was his wife. There are life situations not unlike that, and they are not laughing matters. What are we to make of people who look the picture of health but are so afraid of illness that they dose themselves with a succession of drugs advertised as preventive? What are we to make of the person who has established himself and is accounted a success by all who know him, yet is never at peace with himself because, though others believe in him and in his capacity and competence, he does not believe in himself but lives in fear of failure and keeps driving himself restlessly from one achievement to another. Nobody knows better than he does how hagridden he is by his fears, and his fears are absurd and ridiculous. As though there were not hobgoblins in plenty in the world he has to manufacture them and wear himself out in the process. Doctors, psychiatrists, ministers are constantly encountering men and women who cannot live with a quiet mind because they are at the mercy of terrors which exist in their imagination. Because they exist only in the imagination it will not do to say that they are groundless or unreal. They are fantastic, but never make out that they are not real when they are so obviously tormenting their victims by day and torturing them by night.

What has to be borne in mind is that there are natural fears and neurotic fears. If I were tramping through the heart of an African jungle I should very naturally and properly be afraid of snakes. If in my Riverside Drive apartment I were living in terror of snakes under the carpet I would be at the mercy of a fear that is neurotic. The distinction can be a helpful one. Natural fear, like pain, is one of the sentinels of life. Its function is to give us warning of the approach of danger so that we may be on our guard. If we had no fear at all we should probably pay for the lack of it with our lives. Someone has said that rightly used, fear is the father of courage and the mother of safety. Plato taught the youth of Athens that fear and reverence were the two guardians of the ideal state. During World War II a radio commentator, when announcing the number of German fighter planes brought down, fell into the habit of terminating each announcement with the exclamation: "Who's afraid of the Focke-Wulf?" A member of the crew of a Flying Fortress, hearing about the commentator and his exclamation, sent him a picture of his plane and its crew and wrote at the bottom, " 'Who's afraid of the Focke-Wulf?' We are," and signed his name and the names of the entire crew. Were they cowards? On the contrary, they were brave men who realized full well that they were fighting against brave men. Had they known no fear, the wise fear that begets care, it is hardly likely that they would have survived a single encounter.

The fear that is natural puts us on the alert; the fear that is neurotic robs us of resource and paralyzes us. The fear that is natural is a friend; the fear that is neurotic is an enemy, and unless it is managed and mastered we are likely to be wrecked by it. These are days when neurotic fear has grown to such dimensions that it over-shadows the life of multitudes and robs them of both physical and mental health. If there is no salvation from such fear, there is no salvation worthy of the name.

There is no cheap or easy salvation. Life is a difficult and dangerous business. Trouble is a fact in human experience which it is impossible to avoid. Accidents do happen. Fortunes can be lost. So can health. Bereavement will overtake us all some day. There is no point in telling people there is nothing to be frightened at; it is not true. I think of the mother who wanted her boy to run an errand for her. It meant crossing a field in which there was a belligerent goat. The boy was afraid even to enter the field and his mother, deeply imbued with Mental Science and New Thought and their optimistic conclusions, kept saying to him, "But, little son, why should you be afraid? You know that nothing can hurt you. You know that there is no such thing as evil or pain." "Yes," he answered, "I know. But how do I know that the goat knows?" There was sound common sense in his reply. Life is a difficult and dangerous business. Evil and pain are realities. The things that cause fear are never very far from any one of us. It is fear itself that must be met and mastered. Was Franklin Roosevelt speaking out of personal experience, his own experience of physical pain and affliction, when he made the remark that has so often been quoted since, "The only thing we have to fear is fear itself."?

How is it to be managed and mastered? I offer four suggestions. The first is that we make a practice of looking fairly and squarely at our fears. It is a mistake to try to take no account of them. Nor is suppression, the bottling up of anxiety, a cure. As a matter of fact, the attempt to drive a fear from the mind may actually establish it in the mind, pushing it down more and more deeply into the subconscious where, because we have never really come to terms with it, it festers and a condition is created more distressing than that with which we had originally to reckon. Never bluff yourself about your fears. Get them out into the open. Dr. J. A. Hadfield, the Harley Street specialist, instead of telling the shell-shocked soldier to try and forget the war, found that he could cure him by deliberately taking him back in memory to the battle-ground and getting him to recognize what he had all along been loath to admit, that he was afraid. Psychologically, the healthy soldiers were the men who were not above admitting that they were frightened under combat; they "exteriorized" rather than "repressed" their fear. The best way to get rid of a tune in the head is to sing it out of the head. The best way to be rid of a repugnant desire is not to refuse to acknowledge its existence, but to accept it for what it is and bid it be gone. To know the facts is not weak-ness but wisdom. The refusal to face the reality of fear is more dangerous than fear itself. So I suggest that you take your fears one by one and have it out with them. The light being clear, you may find them smaller than you thought. And some of them, under cross-examination, may disappear.

The second suggestion I have to make is this: Many of our fears are to be traced directly to self-interest. If there was less self-seeking on our part we should be less fretful and fidgety. Do you recall one of the questions which Emily, in Thornton Wilder's play *Our Town*, brought back with her from the other world?—"Are we always at the mercy of one self-centred passion or another?" Most of us are for the greater part of the time. We want health and wealth and happiness and success, and if there is one thing we are afraid of more than another it is that they may not come our way, or that having come our way, they may be snatched from us. The real root of our fear is that we are too much wrapped up in our-selves. Our scale of values is wrong and we know, for our hearts tell us, that God gives no assurance that the things we are seeking, our own comfort and material security, will be guaranteed to us. It is not our comfort with which God is concerned but our character.

Only when our hearts are centred on the things that really matter can we be free from care.

No one ever stated this more plainly than Jesus. He said that he had come to show men the secret of life, life with power and joy in it and free from frustration and fear. When we ask, "What is the secret, his secret?" the answer we get turns a searchlight in on our motives and purposes, for it is that we must say No to self. "Let a man deny himself"—that was his first demand. It is a terribly difficult thing even to try to do. How many of us succeed in the attempt or persist with it? Let us frankly acknowledge, what all experience proves is the fact, that it somehow goes against the grain to put God first and others next and ourselves last. Yet in proportion as the thing is done a blow is dealt at self-centredness, the root of so many of our fears, and we find ourselves on the high road to serenity and stability.

I turn now to a third suggestion for the management and mastery of fear. It is so familiar that the chances are you may dismiss it as platitudinous and conventional and deny it the consideration it really merits. Have you ever prayed about your fears, spread them out before God, told Him about them, naming them over one by one, acknowledging how they leave you inhibited and frustrated, beseeching Him to rid your heart and mind of them? Answers to prayer depend largely on what we pray for. People pray for health and sickness is their portion, or for success and it does not come their way. I have never known of any person who has prayed earnestly and honestly for courage to stand up to life and its demands who has not risen from his knees with fresh heart and hope. Fear cannot be conquered without courage. Courage is the indispensable virtue. The ancients thought it the chief virtue and the root of all the virtues. Yet the finest courage can be worn down unless it is supported and fortified by something beyond courage. What that something is Paul indicates in a memorable sentence: "Never be anxious, but always make your requests known to God in prayer and supplication with thanksgiving; so shall God's peace, that surpasses all your dreams, keep guard over your hearts and minds in Christ Jesus." Have you ever acted on that suggestion? Have you ever taken your fears to God, got the horizons of Eternity about them, looked at them in the light of His love and grace?

All of which leads up to a final suggestion. If we school ourselves to remember that we are in God's hands—if more and more He becomes a reality to us and we believe more and more in His love—we shall get on top of our fears and achieve the victory over them. The supreme remedy for fear is faith. The pictures that our anxieties paint for us in days like these are not imaginary. We are confronted with problems and perils, with challenges and crises. Crushing economic forces devastate the lives of millions. Hate and suspicion in such a close-knit world as this are full of danger to us all. If we had to face to-morrow and the problems of to-morrow unaided and alone, depending solely on our own reserves and resources, we might well be driven to despair, as some have been driven who have no invisible supports to which to turn. But we are not alone. Beside us and within us can come the Presence that is behind the universe, with wisdom to guide us, strength to protect us, love to keep us to the end. That wise and loving Presence, always taking the initiative, waits for our response. God will never do for any of us what we are too indolent to do for ourselves. But given the response, the result is never in doubt. The fight may be hard and long but victory is sure.

Do you believe that? If you do believe it, do you put your belief into practice? When fear is plaguing you, do you pull yourself up and say quietly, "I believe in God"? When he came to write his autobiography Joseph Fort Newton found himself summing up in a few short sentences his message as a Christian minister. This was what he wrote:

> My message has been very simple. To live well we must have a faith to live by, a self to live with, and a work to live for—something to which we can give ourselves and thus get ourselves off our hands.
>
> We cannot tell what may happen to us in this strange medley of life. But we can decide what happens in us—how we take it, what we do with it—and that is what really counts in the end.
>
> Life is an adventure of faith, if we are to be victors over it, not victims of it. Faith in the God above us, faith in the infinite soul within us, faith in life and in our fellow-souls—without faith, the plus quality, we cannot live.

A sentence from the Book of the Psalms sums up in even briefer form the secret of serenity: "What time I am afraid, I will trust in the Lord."

Isn't It Enough To Be Decent?

SOME TIME ago a student with whom I was talking about religion asked, But what does religion matter as long as one is decent? He is representative of a growing class of persons to-day. They have little or no interest in theology or worship or what goes on generally in churches. Belief, they say, is a side issue, secondary and unimportant. Behaviour is what really matters. Whether we choose one religion or another, or dispense with religion altogether, is of little consequence, so long as we do what is right, honour our undertakings, keep within the bounds of respectability, live a useful life. This is a temper strengthened by the secularism of the age and by the pragmatism native to Americans. We like the simplicity of doing good. To concentrate on action is to avoid wrestling with beliefs and coming to grips with the problems they present. It is a convenient substitute for going to church and saying one's prayers and working out a faith that is one's own. It releases us from all deep thinking about the mystery of existence —death and pain and evil. So one hears it said, Why bother about the complexities of religion? Isn't it enough to be decent?

It is certainly something. Two world wars have smashed moral standards just as viciously as they have levelled cities. From country after country comes a uniform report—the disruption of political, economic and family life has brought about a kind of moral anarchy which is breeding selfishness, lawlessness and crime. Anything that is not tied down, locked up or guarded is apt to change hands without notice. A licentious mode of life is not only common but sought after by great sections of the public. Travellers from overseas bring back depressing accounts of corruption and graft, robbery and violence, thieving children, baby-faced prostitutes. It is not pleasant to talk about these things but it is culpable to ignore them. Said a Frenchman who knows France from end to end, "France's trouble is a matter of morals and morale." It is the universal trouble. The state of morals around the world does not make a pretty picture. Some consider that our civilization is approaching the licence and decadence which characterized Roman civilization in the period of its decline and fall. These certainly are days when it is something to be decent.

Nor can we in America afford to be complacent. Our economic and social life has suffered less disruption than that of most nations but our moral standards have not gone unaffected. This country is no stranger to corruption and graft, robbery and violence. Here, too, traditional standards and values, however much they may be eulogized on commemorative occasions, are under siege. The number of people who are without codes and without inhibitions is increasing. The continuity of the Christian tradition shows signs of wearing thin and the vital succession is in danger of being impaired. Every year more and more young people are going out to meet life with no religious memories or traditions or sanctions behind them. Every year more and more people are joining the ranks of those who say that morality is like religion, an optional matter of personal preference; if that is how you want to live, well and good, but you have no right to impose your wishes on others. The Kinsey Report, which one reviewer predicted would sweep away more illusions, superstitions and hypocrisies than any single work of modern times, but which aroused nothing like the ethical revulsion that was anticipated, did one thing; it brought home to the American public—what had long become apparent to careful observers—that with many it is a commonplace to disregard the Christian moral law. Their behaviour reveals that there are no conventions, no taboos, no revelations which they feel they must accept. With the sense of moral obligation so slack it is certainly something to be decent, if by being decent one means refraining from lying or cheating or fornication, or, more positively, having standards of ethical behaviour and adhering to them, recognizing that there are things that are "done" and things that are not "done." Once at a bachelor party a man prefaced the smutty story he was about to tell with the remark: "No ladies present, I think?" "No," said his host, "but there are some gentlemen." The tale was not told. If that is what is meant by being decent who will make light of it?

But is decency self-sustaining? What does it feed on? Has it any roots? There is a conversation in John Galsworthy's novel *Maid in Waiting* which has a bearing on this. Dinny is talking about religion with her mother and says: "Providence is too remote, Mother. It's too remote. I suppose there is an eternal plan, but we are like gnats for all the care it has of us." "Don't encourage such feelings, Dinny," replies the mother, "they affect one's character." "I don't see the connection between beliefs and character," answers Dinny. "I'm not going to behave any worse because I cease to believe in Providence or in an after life. . . .If I'm decent it's because decency's the decent thing and not because I'm going to get anything by it." One respects that. But the mother's final rejoinder goes to the heart of the matter. "Yes, but why is decency the decent thing if there is no God?"

Unless decency is rooted in the nature of things, unless it is bound up with principle and conscience and has eternal foundations in a moral order, it will be at the mercy of the fluctuating currents of thought and fashion to which men are exposed. It will not hold them "East of Suez, where there ain't no Ten Commandments." It will break down under conditions of stress and strain. That is why war exposes the hollowness of many respectabilities. Sometimes life in a great city does it. Away from familiar surroundings and the loyalties associated with them, in an environment where there is nothing like the solicitude you knew back home as to how you live or what you do, and where there are companions who are openly throwing off the old habits of self-restraint, standards of behaviour, unless they are grounded on conviction and on religious insights and imperatives, are likely to be compromised or surrendered. If our decency consists of emotional preferences built up in us by a particular social environment, if it has no deeper root, the impact on it of an unfamiliar social environment will sorely test it and may bring about its collapse.

Why is decency the decent thing if there's no God? That goes to the heart of the matter because far too many people, decent, well-doing, upright people are content to draw, and draw heavily, on inherited spiritual capital. They themselves make no religious profession. They seldom go to church. They rarely kneel to pray. The Bible is for them a closed book. It is the kind of situation that makes one ask: How long will the decency last if the religious faith continues to decline, and if the decline reaches out to and affects, as it appears to be doing, an ever-widening circle of people in all ranks of life? Will it continue on its own momentum? Is it self-sustaining? There may be adequate moral reserves for the needs of one generation, but what about the next generation? What Dinny's mother was urging was that there is a connection between religion and morality. Sooner or later an irreligious nation becomes an immoral nation. History demonstrates that a decay of religion is generally followed by a deterioration of morals. This is the thesis to which Sir Richard Livingstone keeps returning in all his lecturing and writing. He urges it on the British people in season and out of season as one who believes that their salvation depends on it. And what he has to say is not without relevance for us in America. We have fine material to work on—a variety of racial strains, a sound national character which is being hammered out through the years on the anvil of history. In the past, spiritual forces, of which Christianity is the chief, have done much to control and direct the country, but these forces, which at all times fight an uphill battle, have lost ground; and in proportion as they lose it, life loses direction and purpose, and character becomes a habit whose roots are dead, a house whose foundations are sapped. Here is our biggest need; the need of values and standards which are more than mere habits, which go down below the soil of custom into the rock of clear conviction and are founded on a philosophy of life.

We have to reckon to-day with people who are living on inherited moral capital. Some of them not only do not profess religious faith, they claim to be able to dispense with it, and not infrequently they repudiate it. Talk to them about their irreligion and they ask whether they are inferior in character and integrity to those who are religious. What they disregard is that they are members of a society permeated for generations by religious influences, and that the integrity to which they point and in which they take such pride is part of the social heritage into which it was their good fortune to be born. Many of them were brought up in homes where religion was a living thing and in the impressionable and formative years were profoundly influenced by the external helps to character which such religion provides. Surely we are entitled to say to them:

> You criticize the soil? It reared this
> tree,
> This broad life and whatever fruits it
> bears.

The moral life of many who have cut themselves adrift from religion was nourished by religion. The question is whether the logic of the situation will not work itself out and morality go the way of religion. Isn't that what is happening round the world? The moral capital of society is being heavily overdrawn. Men and women are living on it but subscribing nothing to it. In every land there has been a decline in religion—in faith in God and God's government of the world. With what result? In the wake of the decay of religion there has followed a deterioration of morals —violence, corruption, bad faith, cruelty, want of integrity. Those who ask whether it is not enough to be decent should put to themselves another question, the question put to Dinny by her mother, "Why is decency the decent thing if there is no God?"

That goes to the heart of the matter for one more reason. *Beliefs determine behaviour.* It used to be fashionable to minimize their importance. If a man lives as he should, people would say, does what he happens to believe matter? The stress was on action rather than conviction, on conduct rather than creed, on decency rather than dogma. There was a refusal to treat belief seriously or to allow that it influenced character to any observable degree. It was regarded as something taken over without scrutiny as part of the legacy of the past, handed on to a man by his forbears like a set of family jewels, a static and external heritage to be kept in some ecclesiastical safe-deposit vault and taken out and viewed on high days like Christmas and Easter. What was overlooked was that if a man takes his beliefs seriously they put a stamp on his behaviour, determine what he thinks right and what wrong,

constitute the most significant aspect of his life. Said Thomas
Carlyle with characteristic perspicacity, "The thing a man does
practically believe (and this is often enough without asserting it
even to himself, much less to others); the thing a man does practically lay to heart and know for certain, concerning his vital relations to this mysterious Universe, and his duty and destiny there,
that is in all cases the primary thing for him, and creatively deter-
mines all the rest."

The trouble is that what people believe is not always what they
think they believe. Hypocrisy about belief is woefully common and
is often unconscious. People pay lip service to God and goodness
and think they believe in them, whereas all they believe in is the
necessity of earning $5,000 or $10,000, or $50,000 a year. Beliefs are
indicated, not by verbal assent to this or that proposition, but by
the order in which we strive for things. They are overwhelmingly
important because they are decisive for behaviour. A case like that
of Adolph Hitler explodes the antiquated notion that belief is of
no consequence. If it is a belief held with passion, as was true of
Hitler, it can shape and fashion the lives of millions. Or to take an
instance of a different sort, little did the assistants in the British
Museum who handed out books to Karl Marx know what was going
on in his mind. Who can measure the impact of beliefs quietly
excogitated in the middle of last century on millions of lives to-day?
In face of such facts it is absurd for anyone to maintain that
behaviour is what really matters and that belief is a side issue,
secondary and unimportant. Ultimately behaviour depends on
beliefs. America's biggest need to-day is moral standards and values
which are reflected in behaviour because they are rooted in religious conviction.

Isn't it enough to be decent? No, it is not enough. And not only
for the reasons I have advanced. The attitude back of the question
is too negative, too minimal, too prudential. It reminds one of the

schoolboy who asked his minister, What is the least that a Christian must believe? Jesus said something to his disciples in that connection that we should get into the foreground of our thinking. "Except your righteousness shall exceed the righteousness of the Scribes and Pharisees, you shall not enter into the Kingdom of God." It is a plus attitude to life that is required—not the least we can do but the most. Who that has caught sight of what Jesus stands for can be content merely to be decent? Once a man has fallen under the lure and spell of the spirit of Jesus he will not think it meritorious to have fulfilled the legal requirement, he will not cease to run because he has reached the measured mile.

There is a striking paragraph in General Eisenhower's book *Crusade in Europe*. "My brother was already in war work in the government and his hours were scarcely less exhausting than mine. Yet every night when I reached their house, regardless of the hour, which averaged something around midnight, both would be waiting up for me with a snack of midnight supper and a pot of coffee. *I cannot remember ever seeing their house in daylight during all the months I served in Washington*." That is the spirit. It doesn't count hours, or reckon by much or little. It is the spirit of complete devotion and dedication to a great task. There is nothing negative, or minimal or prudential about it. Its strength stands in its sacrifice. Do you wonder that William James said we must find a moral equivalent for war? Get that spirit into the spheres of morality and religion, of behaviour and belief, and you will scorn to ask whether it is enough to be decent. You will say with Philip Doddridge:

> My gracious Lord, I own Thy right
> To every service I can pay,
> And count it my supreme delight
> To hear Thy dictates and obey.

How Does One Get On Top of Irritability and Depression?

We are all familiar with irritability and depression. It is safe to say that there is no one who has not been plagued by them. In one form or another and at one time or another they constitute a problem for each of us. We grow tense, nervy, temperamental, are easily upset by little things, have outbursts of temper out of all proportion to the original stimulus. We have low moods and grey days when we are a nuisance to ourselves and to everybody about us, when nothing is right and everything is a source of annoyance—the world is in a hopeless mess, the government is intolerable, our work lacks interest, other people are wearisome and we lose faith in ourselves.

I speak of irritability *and* depression because they are so often found together. A depressed person is liable to be an irritable person. Low moods and short tempers are rarely far apart. Haven't you noticed that it is when you are "down in the dumps" that you are more than usually sensitive, touchy, petulant? And conversely, an irritable person is liable to be a depressed person. I have heard an outburst of temper defended as "letting off steam." I have known irascible individuals for this reason claim that swearing makes them better-tempered. This is mostly self-deception and rationalization. During the war a soldier who was driving a car occupied by a chaplain nearly caused a general's car to swerve into a ditch. The chaplain was summoned to the general's side and received the full force of an explosion of rage. He had never been so eloquently cursed, and not being allowed to answer back, he could observe the progress of the paroxysm. The general let off steam for a solid three minutes, and the more he said the angrier he became. He only stopped at last because he was so angry that he literally couldn't speak. That sort of tirade does not make for peace of mind or equanimity of disposition. The person who lets his temper run wild does not find it comfortable to live with himself. Give way to irritability and it won't be long before you have to reckon also with depression.

Between them they work a great deal of havoc with human happiness. Far more than most of us realize they spoil lives and embitter relationships. They lead to coolness, resentment, estrangement. They make parents a trial, and sometimes a terror, to their children. They have been the beginning of the end of marriages that otherwise might have been happy. People who give way habitually to irritability and depression deplete themselves both of strength and serenity. They become disinclined for effort and find it hard to believe in the worth of the work they are doing. The trouble may run deeper. It may result in want of faith in themselves, in their fellows, in life, in God. Nor is the mischief confined to themselves. Wasn't it Goldsmith who, in *The Deserted Village,* described a class of children anxiously marking at the start of the day and at his first entrance to the classroom the mood of the teacher, knowing well and by experience that on that so much depended? Depression and irritability are acutely infectious. They spread themselves like pests in homes, classrooms, offices, workshops.

What about their cause? It may be *physical*. Nothing is more delicate and subtle than the interrelation and the interaction of the body and the soul, and sometimes lack of zest for life, irritability and depression are due to inattention to hygiene and the want of good fresh air. That is one of the reasons why the Church must wage a constant war against slums and slum conditions. When men and women are badly nourished and badly clothed and have to live and sleep in a vitiated atmosphere is it any wonder that they fall into the clutches of Giant Despair? There is a creed of hygiene; there is a religion of sanitation; there is a morality of diet. It is a duty, not only as a rational being but as a Christian, to maintain oneself in health and soundness of body. Eating and drinking, sleeping and waking and exercise are not outside the province of religion; they are as much a part of religion as prayer and worship and daily work, and they vitally affect temper and temperament and our whole way of looking at the world. A healthy body makes for a healthy mind. It is essential to the finest and fullest kind of life. What a different world it would be if men and women, especially in and after the forties, would take more care of their health in general. It used to be suggested that despising the body was the mark of a religious man. Actually it is a profanity. "Know ye not," says Paul, "that your body is the temple of the Holy Spirit?"

Perhaps there is something in that for you. Your low spirits may be due to nothing more than want of exercise, the lack of sunshine and fresh air. Why not get into the open more? In the Gospels we read of Jesus doing so at every opportunity. At nightfall, or before dawn was in the sky, he slipped away from crowded city streets to some quiet garden or to a hillside to rest his soul on God. He seems always to have had perfect physical health. We read of his being spent and weary but never of any kind of sickness. The records indicate that his body was a splendid medium for his spirit.

Irritability and depression may have not a physical but a *mental* source. We do well in this connection to listen to the psychiatrists. They tell us about people who are edgy and gloomy for no other reason than *because they are too busy*. Their sin is the sin of overwork. The pressure is harder and the pace swifter than they have any right to allow them to be. The consequence is that they are everlastingly trying to catch up with arrears of correspondence or social obligations. They are so diligent in the pursuit of their work that they practically sacrifice everything to it. They have no leisure. They scarcely know their own children—at least, with any degree of intimacy. They have no time to trim the lamp of friendship. They drive themselves so hard that they become strained and tired, and then, and inevitably, irritable and depressed. Such people need to be reminded that the half may be more than the whole, and that there is real danger of wrecking nerves and health and happiness by being over-busy and by the folly which refuses to recognize that there are very strict and definite limits which no man may with impunity transgress.

Psychiatrists tell us too about people who are short in their temper and subject to fits of depression *because they are immature*. Behind the mask of many a grown-up face there is a sulky child who wants to cry and be rude because he cannot have his own way. There is the man who finds that breakfast is not ready when he happens to be ready and who is at once crochety and cantankerous about it. He makes a mountain out of a mole-hill and works up a domestic crisis over a trifle. There is the woman of fifty summers and more who weeps her eyes out because her name has been inadvertently omitted from the list of committee members. Such people show by their tantrums that, whatever their height in inches, emotionally, they have not grown up. They are specimens of arrested development. Like small children, they make themselves the centre of their world. Immature is the only word that describes their case. John Wesley stayed once with a man the chimney of whose living room did not work properly so that he was bothered at times with a down-draught which filled the room with smoke. "This is my cross, Mr. Wesley," he whimpered, "this is my cross." The blasphemy of it! To suggest a comparison between a smoking chimney and the Cross on which our Lord suffered and bled and died.

You must have overheard, as I have done, a conversation taking some such turn as this. "Do you remember that old black hat she was wearing?" "Yes, perfectly well, but it wasn't black, it was brown." "No, it was black, I can see it as clear as a picture." "Well, I am absolutely positive it was brown." "You can say so if you like, but that won't alter the fact. I have a particularly good memory for colours." "Well, you needn't get mad about it anyway!" Each retort increases the anger of the other party and so, out of a clear sky, has come a ridiculous quarrel. As if it mattered what the colour of the hat was! How utterly futile! How utterly childish! But how high in misery-making potential!

Psychiatrists tell us also about people whose irritability and depression *are principally due to self-absorption, to too intent a preoccupation with their own interests and pleasures.* What they need is to forget themselves and go out and do something kind to somebody. Dean Inge puts it in this way: "Doctors are fond of sending their fashionable patients to take a rest-cure. In nine cases out of ten, a work-cure would do them far more good. . . . The happy people are those who are producing something; the bored people are those who are consuming much and producing nothing." Incidentally, that is why rest and quiet are seldom good cures for depression. "Go and lie down" in most cases is bad advice. It is when he gets us down that Giant Despair keeps us down, or tries to. He works on our gloom and magnifies our fears. There is one way to defeat black moods and tempers; it is to get out into the open, find a cause that will keep us active, absorb ourselves in the interests and needs of our fellows, acquire real fatigue in place of imagined exhaustion. In the real world we forget our self-pitying moods. When we see what others have to suffer we become ashamed to mention our petty troubles. Depression cannot live under the same roof with honest, well-regulated activity. When John Bright sat in grief and gloom mourning the death of his young wife, Richard Cobden went to him—it was during the first terrible years of the Industrial Revolution—and after addressing to him words of condolence, said: "There are thousands of homes in England at this moment where wives, mothers and children are dying of hunger. When the first paroxysm of your grief is past I would advise you to come with me, and we will never rest till the Corn Law is repealed." The mood of depression was mastered by response to the call of duty. Bring happiness into the lives of others and you will not be able to keep it out of your own.

Irritability and depression may have a *spiritual* rather than a physical or mental source. They may be due to sin, to soul sickness, to what the psychologists call "conscience distress." Shakespeare describes it in *Macbeth*, as Nathaniel Hawthorne does in *The Scarlet Letter*. There are even more notable descriptions in the 51st Psalm and in the seventh chapter of Romans. There is no dejection like that of the man whose conscience is accusing and plaguing him. Nothing so frays the nerves or frets the soul as the knowledge that one is habitually falling below self-imposed standards and ideals. To pretend that wrong is right, to do wrong instead of right, is to find yourself just as much frustrated as if you flouted a law like the law of gravity. A man can take blow after blow from life and come up smiling provided his heart is clean and his record honourable. The chances and changes of existence may do him hurt, but the most grievous injuries are those that are wrought by remorse, by the memory of wrongs unatoned, by temptations against which a definite stand is not made, by the presence, day in day out, unwelcome but persistent, of unsubdued sins. Those are the forces that sow the seeds of despondency and irritability in the soul.

> Canst thou not minister to a mind diseased,
> Pluck from the memory a rooted sorrow,
> Raze out the written troubles of the brain,
> And with some sweet oblivious antidote
> Cleanse the stuff'd bosom of that perilous stuff
> Which weighs upon the heart?

How short-sighted we often are in dealing with what in the final reckoning are spiritual maladies! How superficial is our diagnosis of much of our heaviness and depression! The poverty of our resources may be seen in the remedies we propose. Change of air. Change of scene. Change of diet. Change of interest. A round of gaiety and merry-making. They all have been tried, and they all have their value. But for the deeper maladies of the soul, for the individual who has lost the sense of God and is without his bearings on the ocean of life, who wants to be something that he seems powerless to be, who is mastered by temptation and dogged by moral failure, they are the merest quackery and do no more than tinker with the disease. When John Henry Newman was a university student and in spiritual distress, and his letters home lacked their usual vivacity, his mother wrote to him, "Your father and I fear very much from the tone of your letters that you are depressed. We fear that you debar yourself a proper quantity of wine." Poor woman! Her boy was fighting for his soul and all that she could recommend was a stimulant for his body.

That sort of thing happens everyday. People who are restless and rootless and at an end of themselves, whose heart and flesh are crying out for the living God, are recommended to try a cocktail, or to betake themselves to the theatre, or to forget their worries in an absorbing novel. Time and again it happens that by such measures their unrest is only aggravated. External remedies may do no more than benumb the senses as when a man turns to drink or sedatives, hoping thereby to forget his failure and drown his misery. At best they afford only a temporary respite. No one knows that better than the victim himself. The gloom settles down again and like a fog envelops the soul.

Where is the true and lasting remedy for such maladies to be found? If you want something against which you can lean your back and know that it will never give, you must have a living religion. You must learn to stay your soul on God. You must ask Him to provide the inner resources you lack—ability to pull yourself together, a faith to live by, a faith to live for, a spiritual source of maturity and integrity and victory. Long ago a man in deep depression asked: "Why art thou cast down, O my soul? And why art thou disquieted within me?" He went about the business of making a diagnosis. But he did not stop with a diagnosis. He made for himself a prescription: "Hope thou in God, for I shall yet praise Him who is the health of my countenance and my God." It is a prescription deserving of consideration for it comes to us tested and validated in generation after generation by men and women who found it a sovereign remedy. If in what I have been saying I have been diagnosing your need, here is the first thing and the best thing for you to do. Do not omit the Invisible in your reckoning. By all means listen to what doctors have to say about bodily health and to what psychiatrists have to say about mental health, but remember that the soul of all improvement is the improvement of the soul. For that you need God. To try to live without Him is to be restless and rootless. If you are to see clearly and act wisely and live happily and courageously you must learn to stay your soul on God.

Why Can't We Learn To Live Together?

Most of the problems of life have to do with the difficulty of living together. Pick up the newspaper any morning and as you read it your first thought might well be that human beings have an almost infinite capacity for disagreeing with one another. Chinese Nationalists and Chinese Communists; Moslems and Hindus in India; Jews and Arabs in Palestine; employers, employees and various governmental agencies in this country; Soviet Russia and her satellites versus the outside world—it is a depressing picture.

And the dissension extends into smaller units—business offices, college faculties, social clubs, families. To live together sweetly, graciously, harmoniously, in spite of prickles of temper and peculiarities of disposition, is not easy. Great numbers of people find that even to make a tolerable success of marriage and family life is a whole time occupation. The intimate, day-by-day, elbow-rubbing relationships of life make a heavy demand. We don't instinctively like everybody we meet, not even all the good people we meet; and we may be sure there are poeple who find it difficult to like us. The problem of living together, the failure of all of us in varying degree to solve that problem, runs through every area and level of life, from the difficulties parents have with their children and children with their parents right up to the wide-spread dissension and consequent confusion of the international situation to-day. Why can't we learn to live together?

The harm that is done by the almost infinite capacity of mankind for disagreeing with itself beggars description. For sheer misery-producing power dissension has no equal. It embitters life, destroys its most sacred relationships, devastates homes, breaks up communities, leads ultimately to wars with millions of young men slain, women's hearts broken, babies starved, minds rendered insane. A girl of eighteen told her minister that her parents had not spoken to each other for several years. They communicated with each other, she said, by notes or by messages conveyed through the children. Think of the misery-producing power of a situation like that. And the origin of the quarrel was whether a certain Mr. and Mrs. Jones should or should not be invited to dinner!

What a humourless, juiceless pair they must have been. Part of their trouble surely was that they took themselves too seriously, were bereft of any glimmering of fun, had never learned to look in the mirror and laugh at themselves. There is a lot of homely, practical wisdom in the saying of an old Negro preacher: "If you could jist set on the fence and see yourself pass by, you'd die laughing at the sight." To live happily and harmoniously with ourselves we have to learn to know ourselves; we have to try to reason with ourselves; we have to be able to laugh at ourselves. To live happily and harmoniously with others we have to teach ourselves to see the amusing side of a situation; we have to cultivate a sense of humour, gentle, genial and unsoured. I am not talking about satire or sarcasm for they can wound and leave scars. I am not talking about wit for it can be biting and bitter. I am talking about humour that is kindly and cordial and large-hearted.

Such humour, for example, as Spurgeon's who said of some difficult people in his congregation: "They must have been sent into the world, not that I might save their souls, but that they might discipline mine." Such humour as Bishop Creighton's, who with the same sort of persons in mind, said: "Whenever you have got the ape and the tiger out of people there still remains the donkey, a much more stubborn animal." Henry Ward Beecher once received a letter containing the single word "Fool." He told his congregation about it, but not to rouse their ire or gain their sympathy, for this was what he went on to add, "I have known many an instance of a man writing a letter and forgetting to sign his name, but this is the only instance I have ever known of a man signing his name and forgetting to write the letter."

In each case an excellent way of facing up to what might have been a difficult situation. No disposition to complain or to invite sympathy but a sense of humour, rich, deep, sunny. To have such humour is a saving grace. It takes the tension out of life. It removes the irritation and the friction. It saves us from egotism and from going about wearing blinkers. It is strange that religion and the sense of humour should have fallen out so often. It always means the degradation of humour and the impoverishment of religion. One thing is certain. If we are to make headway in the art of living together we have got to have and keep a sense of humour.

And with it the spirit of tolerance. There is a story of George Fox and Oliver Cromwell that is worth recalling. Between them in the matter of religion there was a great barrier. But one day they met and talked about what Carlyle called "the perennials." When Fox got up to go Cromwell said, "If thou and I were but one hour a day together, we should be nearer to the other. I wish no more harm to thee than to my own soul." That is the spirit to nourish and foster. It animated an old man, a devout Methodist, who, when the sound of the Angelus bell was borne on the wind from the Roman Catholic chapel in the neighbouring village, would take off his hat and say, after a moment's silence, "In my Father's house are many mansions." Such a spirit, tolerant, gracious, charitable, offers a basis for happy and harmonious community life. It is more than a mere amenity. It is more positive than forbearance. It means respect for the beliefs, practices and habits of others without necessarily sharing or accepting them. It means protecting the liberties and rights of those from whom one differs. It found classical expression in Voltaire's aphorism, "I disapprove of what you say, but I will defend to the death your right to say it." Given that spirit, you have not only a basis for happy and harmonious community life, but a bulwark of individual and social liberty.

There is another spirit abroad at the present time, the spirit of intolerance and bigotry. It has arisen in an America that is strangely afraid of itself. It is a spirit born of a half-hysterical fear that tends to confuse loyalty with orthodoxy, that insists on the affirmation and reaffirmation of allegiance as though allegiance were something that could be compelled, that is impatient of diversity of outlook and opinion, and that frowns on deviation of any kind. Typical of this new temper was a suggestion made recently to the effect that "just now with the critical condition of this country, anyone about whom there is any question should not be allowed to speak."

An extraordinary sentiment to come from the lips of an American. It represents a new and un-American trend. I think by way of contrast of the ideal Thomas Jefferson held out to prospective teachers at the University of Virginia. "This institution will be based on the illimitable freedom of the human mind. For here we are not afraid to follow truth wherever it may lead, nor to tolerate error so long as reason is free to combat it." I think of the proud claim of Thomas Paine, "This new world hath been the asylum for the persecuted lovers of civil and religious liberty from *every* part of Europe." I think of the speech made by Congressman Page of Virginia in 1790 in support of a liberal naturalization policy. "It is nothing to us whether Jews or Roman Catholics settle among us; whether subjects of Kings, or citizens of free States wish to reside in the United States, they will find it in their interest to be good citizens, and neither their religious nor political opinion can injure us, if we have good laws, well executed." It was tolerance of diversity that made the United States possible. It was tolerance of wide differences in religious faith and racial background and economic interest that enabled this country to absorb and gain enrichment from the hosts of immigrants seeking freedom and opportunity here. It was tolerance that lay at the basis of this nation's life and that made happy, harmonious community life possible. No one can injure America as mortally as Americans, and they can do it by terror-stricken bigotry.

The thing that needs to be said in this connection is that tolerance ought not to mean laxity. Sometimes, it has to be admitted, that is all it does mean—the easy-going temper which is easy-going just because it has no fixed standards of right or wrong. The proper name for this sort of thing is not tolerance but indifference. We cannot afford to let our thinking about tolerance become muddled and confused. It is too precious a possession. It was won only after centuries of effort. Our kind of democracy is impossble without it, and so are a free church and a free pulpit. The trouble is that we incline to take its existence for granted, and we have no right to take its existence for granted. The events of recent years should have taught us once and for all that it is a tender plant and requires constant cultivation. The price of its maintenance is perpetual vigilance. If we want to live together happily and harmoniously and in freedom we shall have to foster and nurture the spirit of tolerance.

We shall need knowledge as well as tolerance. We know far too little about one another. There are too many iron curtains in the modern world. Nothing breeds misunderstanding and intolerance like ignorance. How one wishes one could really know what is going on in the minds of Russians. How one wishes Russians could know more of the real truth about us. Every year a miracle takes place immediately to the north of us in International House. Students live there under the same roof who have come to New York from Europe and Asia and South America. The result is a meeting of minds, a sharing of impressions, the free dissemination of knowledge. To see the other person's point of view, to appreciate how he comes to think and feel as he does, to discover what he has been through, is to be well on the way to a basis of mutual understanding and to the happiest kind of community life.

We shall need imagination as well as knowledge. By imagination I mean the ability intensively and comprehensively to put oneself in another's place and see things from his point of view. "Because I have been athirst," says an Arab proverb, "I will dig a well, that others may drink." It was because of their want of imagination that Job lost patience with his friends. "Will your windy speeches never end?" he asked them. "I could talk as you are talking, if you were in my place." They were healthy and wealthy old men who had not suffered enough to have their shallow orthodoxy ruffled. Instead of being able to sympathize with Job they only hurt and irritated him by reeling off their pious platitudes. You won't get far in your relations with people unless you use your imagination. I like what an old Scotswoman, talking of the boyhood of Professor A. B. Bruce said, "He was a wild laddie, but he wasna' deevilish." That old woman had the gift—it is a gift, the kind of gift one can cultivate—of sympathetic imagination. If we did cultivate it, would the blindness and the blunders be possible which so often embitter life? Would we be content, to take a specific case, to let India's millions face starvation while our granaries are full and running over? Would the people who need help have to go so frequently without it? Would not sickness and sorrow and want be approached with a gentler pity and our whole handling of others be more gracious and generous because we have thought ourselves into their situations, and have put a little imagination into the working of the Golden Rule? The Italians have an excellent proverb: Clear understandings mean long friendships. You can be a true friend only if you deliberately set yourself to see things as others see them, to take a look at the world from their viewpoint.

One other quality at least is needed if we are to live together happily and harmoniously. It is integrity. That is our deepest need today. Integrity is the cement of society; when integrity crumbles civilization collapses. Signs are not wanting that here and there it is crumbling. Our moral sense is at a low ebb. Never surely have self-interest and self-aggrandizement been so naked and unashamed. The happenings and disclosures of recent months have brought home to us that men and women of character and principle are America's top requirement. I heard not long ago of a party of native bearers in Central Africa who suddenly set down their packs and refused to go forward. When asked for the reason, one of them said, "Our bodies have gone too quickly for our souls." We on this Continent ought to take those words to heart. Nothing lies nearer the root of our failure to live in peace and harmony than the fact that our spiritual progress has not kept pace with our technical progress. Science daily puts into our hands greater and still greater powers, but unless there is an advance in moral character to correspond with the technical advance the results are bound to be calamitous. Unless we have finer citizens we are heading for a crash.

After the fatal battle of Culloden Moor, Bonnie Prince Charlie was a hunted fugitive in the Scottish Highlands. For five months

he moved about among the ordinary people, trusting his identity
to fishermen and ghillies, many of whom had no notion where
their next meal was coming from. Any one of them could have
had £30,000, the price the Government put on his head, by disclosing his hiding-place to the nearest English garrison. He was
never betrayed. It is that kind of integrity we must have—men in
government, on the bench, in business, in all walks of life who
can be absolutely depended upon, who will not sell their souls
for cash, whose word is their bond, whose moral sense is sound.
There can be no lasting bond of community without integrity.

Where are we to acquire integrity? How are we to learn to live
happily and harmoniously with others? There is no psychological
technique to compare with the religious discipline. The great
master of the art of living is Christ. The real transformer of life
is Christ. The power that makes and remakes character is the
power of Christ. When men and women come under his influence,
daily lift up their mind and spirit in loyalty to him, get to know
his will and seek his grace to do it, they have found the deepest
bond of community.

Is There an Art to Living in New York City?

I RAISE to-day a question that has repeatedly been put to me. How is one to learn the art of living in New York City? Let me say at once that I recognize that there are people for whom the question poses no problem. They love this city. They have been at home in it since the first day they set foot in it. They have no wish to leave it nor the remotest intention of doing so. In Scotland you will hear it said that every minister cherishes a secret wish—to go to heaven by way of Edinburgh. Neither ministers nor Edinburgh have a monopoly of that kind of ambition. There are men and women by the thousand who are happy to live here and who expect and will be content to die here. For them New York City is a perpetual wonderland—its air sparkling and invigorating, its skyscrapers with their row upon row of lighted windows like fairy palaces, its little shops and restaurants and odd corners unique in their charm, its cosmopolitanism an insistent reminder that this is the crossroads of the world.

Do you think I am overstating the case? Then listen to this from the pen of a one-time resident of Riverside Drive. "Below my window was the lordly, broad-breasted Hudson. Its moods were as many as my own, varying with the hours: now lucid and lovely, now overhung by a soft haze of dreamy meditation, now swept by a blue dust of rain. It became almost personal in its friendliness, and I felt its bafflement as the inflowing tide pushed its waters upstream, like the pressure of the Eternal Will thwarting my impulsive spirit, like the struggle in the heart of Everyman. Every evening the Divine Artist painted a sunset scene over the New Jersey hills, and I marvelled at His masterpieces. One evening haunts me still. The whole sky was aglow with gorgeous colours, a mass of molten splendour like Dante's rose of gold, with foundations of dark vapour. Gradually the gold changed to delicate, tender green, then to pale lavender, deepening into soft purple as night came down, like a shade drawn over a latticed window in the City of God." I ask you: What does a man like that need to learn about the art of living in New York?

Yes, but the picture has another side. There are people who do not love this city. They are not at home in it. They live and work and bring up their children here, but their hearts are not here. Cyrus McCormick of Chicago whose grain reaper revolutionized farming and brought him almost uncountable wealth was, it is said, so sentimental that he would burst into tears at the mention of his native Virginia. Some New Yorkers are not unlike that. No matter how long they may reside in it, this city will never take pride of place in their affections. It is a capital place in which to make money, but at every opportunity they point the nose of their automobile toward its exits. They do not live in it, unless they have to, and if they have to live in it, at the back of their minds is a secret dream, a dream about the day when they will take their leave of it and live in a house free from soot and grime, with a garden surrounding it and with neighbours who are unhurried and neighbourly.

What is it about New York that gets them down? It is the noise

—raucous and rasping. It is the pace—fast and furious. It is the crowds jamming their way into elevators and subways. It is the artificiality, the feeling that life is standardized, automatic, machine-driven, like the device on Broadway into the slot of which you put twenty-five cents, gaze into a glass, move your head from side to side and look pleasant, then turn a handle and receive your portrait taken in a half-dozen different positions. It is the hardness, the strident go-getting, the unabashed materialism, the competition, with all that they involve in stress and strain. It is the impersonal character of existence, proximity without community, scores of families occupying shelves, not knowing who lives above or below nor caring, so that a man can be carried out in his coffin and the fact of his death be for many of his neighbours the first indication that he had ever lived. Any one of a host of things can make living in New York difficult—bad housing, bad working conditions, poverty of which there is a deal more than is recognized, especially genteel poverty, loneliness, old age, ambitions once tumbling over one another but now unrealized and never to be realized. There are those for whom life under such conditions ultimately seems insupportable. According to a recent Department of Health report, during a five-year period 4,374 New Yorkers committed suicide.

That is part of the picture, though much too sombre a part to dwell on for long. What of the practical aspect of the case? Whether we are fond of it or dislike it we have to learn to live in a city that has two sides to it, the city apostrophized by O. Henry as "like a ragged purple dream, the wonderful, cruel, enchanting, bewildering, fatal, great city." None of those adjectives is exaggerated; none of them is superfluous. New York is like that and to live in it calls for adjustment alike of body and mind.

To make an art of living in it we have to get to know it familiarly and intimately, as one gets to know and love a person. Once when T. H. Huxley was walking over a Scottish moor, he picked up a moss-cup and began to examine it with his pocket lens. A shepherd, moved by curiosity, drew near and watched with interest. Huxley asked him whether he would like to look at the familiar object through the lens. He eagerly assented. As he looked, his eyes dilated with astonishment and presently he said, "Can this be a moss-cup?" Assured that it was, he asked if he might look again; then, handing back the lens and the moss-cup, after a moment's silence, he said, "Sir, I wish you had never shown it to me." "Why?" Huxley asked in surprise. "Because," was the reply, "I tread on thousands of them every day of my life." It may be that what we need is a lens of some kind that will reveal to us the wonder and splendour and beauty of New York. What we require to learn, if it is to appeal to us, is *to take in things through the eyes.* So many walk the city streets and notice nothing, and all the while there is so much to see —the skyscrapers with their fantastic, unearthly, unforgettable beauty; the bridges, of which the mighty Triborough spanning the waters both of the East River and Long Island Sound, serves as an example; the panorama of New York harbour that unfolds itself as for a few cents one makes the crossing from the Battery to Staten Island, and what a panorama—little tugs towing flatboats loaded with railroad cars, a Turkish freighter from Istanbul flying the Star and Crescent, a Cunard liner dwarfing its near neighbours as it makes for the open sea. Simeon Strunsky, who knew this city and loved it, was fond of telling of the traveller from Europe who, catching sight for the first time of our world-famous skyline, turned to a friend and said: "The people of New York go about their work in one vast cathedral of Chartres." The statement is not one that we are likely to take too seriously, but it illustrates my point. To learn the art of living in this city we shall have to be at some trouble to find out what it has to offer, and to find out what it has to offer we shall have to teach ourselves to take in things through our eyes.

The second point I want to emphasize goes deeper. It was suggested by a remark made recently by the French actress, Edith Piaf. "People who do not like New York," she said, "have no heart." I think I know what she meant. Any great-souled person who is a lover of humanity will sooner or later come under the lure of this big city. Its crowds will have for him a certain fascination; its huge cosmopolitanism will fire his imagination. Let me share with you a personal experience. When I first settled in New York nothing so got me down as its crowds, especially the crowds on the subway. To see them at the rush hours in the evening, a swarming, jostling, work-weary multitude, was a depressing business. I spoke of the matter to a well-known minister in the city and he told me something that proved of service to me and may do to somebody here. "My experience," he said, "when I first came to Manhattan ten years ago was identical with yours. The subway filled me with a distaste for my kind. I hated to have to push and be pushed and to find myself cheek by jowl with representatives of half the races under heaven. Then I remembered what I was—a Christian minister—and what I believed and was preaching—that we are all, black, yellow, white, the children of one Father. I began to say to myself, These men and women are my brothers and sisters and life is pressing hard on them. What can I do better than offer a prayer for them? So now," he told me, "the subway is for me an oratory. As I stand straphanging, the uplifted hand is the symbol of the prayer I offer for my fellows." That was two years ago. He has been at work for twelve years now in this city and bids fair to go on for twelve years more. His rich humanity, his love for his fellows, explain his growing affection for New York. I owe it to him to say that he taught me a simple and rewarding lesson.

To have a rich humanity like his we require the other quality he has—a quick and sensitive imagination, the ability to think ourselves into the place of others so that their pains and pleasures come home to us as our own. Teufelsdröckh, as Carlyle describes him in *Sartor Resartus,* in his eyrie on the attic floor of the highest house in the Wahngasse had it and entered in an extraordinary degree into the whole life circulation of the city of Weissnichtwo. Though why should I name Teufelsdröckh when a greater name can be cited? Jesus had it and one does not wonder, with a spirit as sensitive as his, and knowing Jerusalem as he did, its nameless possibilities, its aching pathos, that as he came round the brow of the hill that looked down on the Capital he wept over it. Nor is any one who walks about this city with kindled imagination likely to remain unmoved by it. Taking in things through his eyes—Harlem as well as Park Avenue, the Bowery as well as Broadway, our dark, dismal slums as well as the Waldorf-Astoria—what he sees will do more than hold his interest and prod his conscience; if he has a heart it will touch his feelings. Others may at the first opportunity turn their backs on New York; he will give himself up to its service, believing that nowhere is the need greater or the opportunity more challenging.

Certainly the opportunity is nowhere more challenging. With something like sixty nationalities living within its five boroughs, New York is more representative of the world than the United Nations. The other day the head of a city mission, asked if he had any colleagues, replied that he was obliged to have eleven—all speaking different languages. New York is built on islands, but it is not insular. It has a cosmopolitanism of the mind as well as of colour, class and language. Nothing here is static or stereotyped. One has the feeling as one moves about that history is palpably in the making and a bracing, stimulating feeling it is. Politically, economically, socially, in the sphere of opinions and ideas, it sets the tone and the pace for the rest of the country.

This immediate neighbourhood is the nation's greatest educational and cultural centre. Not only so, with America foremost among the great powers and the United Nations establishing here its permanent home, New York is now as never before the cross-roads of the world. Who would not wish to live his life and do his work in such an absorbing city?

A great deal depends, however, on the character of the work. Too many people come to this city who are interested basically in two things and two things only—living well and making money. And since the first is dependent on the second, and in their interpretation of it unrealizable apart from the second, they make buying and selling and the declaring of dividends a kind of religion. The acquisitive instinct brought them here and keeps them here. Having its way with them, lording it over them year after year, it turns them out in case after case "vulgar of manner, overfed, overdressed and underbred." During the Civil War, Anthony Trollope visited New York and afterwards in *Barchester Towers* wrote: "Free institutions, general education and the ascendancy of dollars are the words written on every paving stone along Fifth Avenue, down Broadway, and up Wall Street. Every man can vote, and values the privilege. Every man can read, and uses the privilege. Every man worships the dollar, and is down before his shrine from morning to night."

That sort of thing—and to-day there is far more of it than when Trollope wrote—pays dividends of a kind; it does not make for the deepest happiness. A man may live well in the sense that he may have a luxurious home, a lavish table and cellar and the means of gratifying every physical desire, yet he may know next to nothing about the art of living. He may be edgy and restless and with all his money-making profoundly dissatisfied, going about with a look in his eyes that suggests he has lost something, and knows he has lost it but that he is uncertain what it is or how to lay hold on it. Have you noticed how many visitors to New York go away registering the same impression—that though the richest city in the world, ours is not a happy city, that there are too many people in it crowding one another and competing with one another, their unease and disquiet apparent in all their motions, their frustration and disillusionment written on their faces for all to see?

If you have come to New York to get rather than to give, to serve your own ends rather than the common good, to establish and make a name for yourself, you are on the wrong track. You may achieve your goal, but I warn you that if you do, there will be bitterness as well as sweetness in your cup. To struggle for your own hand, to be smart, alert, vigilant solely in your own interest is to make a sorry bungle of the art of living. That applies anywhere, but it especially applies here. There is a more excellent way. Put in the place of the desire for private gain the motive of service and make it the mainspring of your existence. You are going to be a doctor? Be sure you are a doctor who works not for fees but for health, not for your own advancement but for the public good. You are going into business? Carry into it the principles of Jesus and reckon *now* with the possibility that their application in your case may mean that you will never be rich. You are going to be a teacher in school or university? See to it that you do not become a place hunter who does his work with one eye on his salary and the other on the prospects of promotion, but a man or a woman who lives to teach truth, and in that and other ways to mould the lives that come under your influence. New York City would be a happier place if its inhabitants gave less thought to private gain and more to the common good. The first prerequisite for the art of living is a sense of vocation. To have work to do here, work to which one can give head and heart and hand, work that is abundantly worth doing and involves no loss of self-respect is to find the way to the deepest happiness.

Are you having difficulty in coming to terms with this city? I suggest three things. Teach yourself to take in things through your eyes and the wonder, splendour and beauty of New York will begin daily to unfold themselves. Cultivate a love for its people, and with it a sensitive imagination that leads you to identify yourself with them, and living in the crossroads of the world will be an absorbing adventure. Put the service of others above the service of self and you will discover in such service a sense of vocation which will not only enable you to adjust yourself to your environment but to be at home in it.

There is a striking sentence in Paul's letter to the Philippians. "All the saints salute you, chiefly those that are of Caesar's household." There were saints in Caesar's household, though the Caesar referred to, the Emperor Nero, was an unspeakable man. Too much can be made of the influence of environment. We are not like wax, shaped and moulded by pressure from without, having no will power or determination of our own. We are not independent of our surroundings, but we can make an original use of them. The determining factors in life are not external but internal. The good life is never easy; it is always possible. To learn the art of living in New York may be difficult, but it can be done. If in Caesar's household in the first century, why not in this metropolis of the world in the twentieth?

What Should Be the Christian Attitude to Communism?

Sooner or later in times like these any man who regularly occupies a Christian pulpit is bound to say something about Communism. There are two reasons for this. The first has to do with the tremendous impact which Communism is making on the life of the contemporary world. It is working like leaven in Europe, Africa, Asia, and the Americas. Multitudes have embraced it as men once embraced religion; for them it is the most coherent philosophy and the greatest single emotional drive they know. It presents itself both as a way of looking at the world and as a means of transforming it. In other words, it is a faith, a religion, for which men are prepared to sacrifice a career, family ties, allegiance to the land of their birth. If the sense of commitment is the differentiating mark of religion, Communism—one is ashamed to have to say this yet it is incontestable—is the most aggressive and missionary-minded religion in the world to-day.

That suggests the second reason why a Christian minister is under obligation to take stock of it. Before coming to New York it was my business, among other things, to teach comparative religion. The textbooks on the subject tended to follow a common pattern. They listed as possible alternatives to Christianity the historic world religions—Judaism, Mohammedanism, Buddhism, Hinduism. Those are genuine alternatives to Christianity; they are live options; but for Christianity's greatest rival we have to look elsewhere. It is not in the direction of Buddha or Mahomet or Jerusalem or the Bhagavadgita that millions in both hemispheres are turning now. Their eyes are directed eastwards. It is about Karl Marx and Lenin and the Soviet experiment that in country after country the student class, for example, talk long into the night. No one in touch with the realities of the contemporary situation will deny that in the crisis confronting civilization Christianity's most formidable competitor and only serious rival is Communism.

What, then, should be our attitude to Communism? Much will depend on our judgement of its intrinsic character and, for this is equally important, on what we conceive to be the distinctive line of action taken by the Christian religion when it finds itself under attack. There are Christians who are convinced on soul and conscience that Communism is an evil thing; it is atheistic and materialistic, and the means it employs to achieve its ends are immoral. Their attitude is one of uncompromising rejection. We all know people whose reaction to the new religion of Communism resembles that of the Reformers to the old religions. Luther called Mahomet the "devil's worshipper" and denounced the Koran as "brutish and hoggish." In one of his hymns there is a couplet:

> Lord, shield us with Thy Word and hope
> And smite the Moslem and the Pope.

Substitute Kremlin for Moslem and some would sing the lines with gusto. The sentiments and disposition of the first Christian missionaries were no different. Christianity, they contended, was the one true religion; all the others were false, tissues of error and corruption. And not only the first Christian missionaries! Dr. Samuel Johnson once said: "There are two objects of curiosity, the Christian world and the Mohammedan world; all the rest may be considered barbarous." About Communists today there are Christians who permit themselves the use of language just as derogatory and denunciatory. Concerning such a temper we should ask one thing: Granted that a movement is evil, what ought to be the distinctive Christian attitude toward it? Evil must be exposed and opposed but *how*?

I raise the question now and later will come back to it. The thing to keep in mind, if we are to appraise the total picture, is that there are Christians who see Communism in another light and speak of it in other terms. Here is Dr. George A. Coe speaking toward the end of the second World War. "In spite of all the similarities between the regimes of Hitler and Mussolini on the one hand and that of Stalin on the other, there are contrasts as deep as the ocean. . . . The enormous spread of literacy in the Soviets, at a moment when, in Germany and Italy, popular culture is contracting; the unparalleled rise in the status of women in the Soviets at the moment that with bands of iron Germany and Italy are fastening women in a secondary and subordinate status; the expansion of the workingman's personality in the Soviets at the moment when Italy and Germany take away from him such dignity as he had acquired in earlier regimes; the transcending of racialism in the Soviets in contrast to the terrible intensification of it in Germany and Italy. . . . A Christian conscience that endeavours to take a world view of contemporary conditions yet fails to perceive this mountain range within the Soviet landscape is profoundly ambiguous." Take another case. William Temple, the late Archbishop of Canterbury, was a distinguished philosopher and a man of affairs. He was a great Christian as well as a great churchman. From all over Christendom men looked to him for light and leading. He once described Communism as a "Christian heresy." What did he mean by that? He meant that Communism had laid hold on certain truths which are an essential part of the Christian scheme of things and which every Christian should acknowledge and profess, but that it had bound up with them concepts and practices which no Christian can ever acknowledge or profess.

Consider two of the truths basic in Communism which are an essential part of the Christian scheme of things. First, Communism is the story of men aflame with a passionate concern for social justice, resolved to set up on a world-wide scale a new society from which ancient injustices—poverty, oppression, the exploitation of man by his brother-man—shall be purged. Undoubtedly this is one of the reasons why Communism makes such a strong appeal to, and awakens such a spontaneous response in, great masses of underprivileged people all round the world. With a passionate concern for social justice Christians are bound to be in the completest accord. It is implicit in the Christian doctrines of the Fatherhood of God, the Brotherhood of man, the infinite worth of the human soul and explicit in passage after passage of the Bible. When churchmen complained to him of the revolutionary sentiments in the Communist song called "The Red Flag," Bishop Gore replied that the Magnificat was no less revolutionary and in illustration quoted from it: "He hath put down the mighty from their seats, and exalted them of low degree. He hath filled the hungry with good things, and the rich He hath sent empty away." Once when a student urged me to read *The Communist Manifesto*—with which I was not unfamiliar for I had been an undergraduate too —we struck a bargain with each other. I undertook to re-read it and he undertook to read—it was apparently to be for the first time— The Manifesto of Jesus, the first recorded sermon he preached, with this for its opening sentence: "The Spirit of the Lord is upon

me, because He hath anointed me to preach the gospel to the poor;
He hath sent me to heal the brokenhearted, to preach deliverance
to the captives, and recovering of sight to the blind, to set at liberty
them that are bruised, to proclaim the acceptable year of the
Lord." A passionate concern for social justice! Nothing less than
a betrayal of essential Christianity would be involved if the Communists had a monopoly of that.

Consider a second conception basic in Communism but also
an integral element in the Christian outlook, the conception of
a classless society. Hitler propagated the theory of a master race.
The Germanic peoples were the *Herren-Volk* and as such were
first to subdue and then to administer all who were of an alien
blood and soil. By contrast Communism envisages a world society
knowing no distinctions of blood or soil, caste or colour. The
Soviets have made anti-Semitism an indictable offence and have
repudiated racism, a factor which in Africa and Asia and among
subject peoples generally accounts for the attraction of Communism as a social theory. But Christian social theory, too, repu-
diates racism. Christianity is a world faith and envisages a world
community in which every partition reared by Facism or Nationalism or Racism has been abolished. It has a charter the terms of
which are strikingly specific: "There is neither Jew nor Greek,
there is neither bond nor free, there is neither male nor female:
for ye are all one in Christ Jesus." In the spirit of that affirmation
we often sing with John Oxenham, having achieved in this congregation in miniature an interracial and international society:

> In Christ there is no East or West,
> In Him no South or North,
> But one great Fellowship of Love
> Throughout the whole wide earth.

The concept of a classless society! No Christian is going to quarrel
with that. Remembering, then, these two concerns—the concern

for social justice and for a world unity in which all barriers of caste and colour are abolished—we approve, I take it, the statement by John Foster Dulles made before the General Conference of the Methodist Church at Boston: "The long-range social ends which Soviet leaders profess are in many respects similar to those which Christians seek."

Why, then, is Communism to which William Temple applied the adjective "Christian" a heresy? Because it is avowedly secularistic and materialistic. It makes no place for God or Christ or for the things Christ put first in life. It is a humanist philosophy in the sense that it expects humanity to usher in by its own unaided efforts the perfect society. It regards religion psychologically as mere wishful thinking, intellectually as the product of fear, ignorance, credulity and superstition, historically as serving the ends of exploiters, whether kings or priests or capitalists. There has of late been some modification of the anti-religious policy of the authorities in Russia where it is said that, despite the fact that atheism is the official policy and education follows a secular pattern, a considerable proportion of the population still publicly affirm their belief in God. Whether the modification is deliberate or due to expediency is a debatable question. Stalin, when he prohibited the Society of the Godless from issuing any further publications, gave as the reason shortage of paper!

Again, Communism is a heresy because it acknowledges no transcendental standards or values. The Communist ethic is completely at loggerheads with the Christian ethic. Since for the Communist there is no Divine government, no absolute moral order, there are no fixed, immutable principles. Communism knows no necessity save that of the class war and no obligations save that of hastening the Revolution. Any means—force, violence, imprisonment, torture, terrorism, lying, murder—justify that millennial end. "We must be ready," wrote Lenin, "to employ trickery, deceit, lawbreaking, withholding and concealing truth." For the sake of the Party and the Cause the Communist must be prepared not only to put aside personal ties and obligations but to override every human consideration and to reduce every moral obligation to the level of sheer expediency. That the followers of Lenin have been willing to act upon his instructions is a matter of history. Harold Laski used to look for inspiration to Moscow as good Christians look to the Bible. He once wrote in a pamphlet: "The Communist Parties outside Russia act without moral scruples, intrigue without any sense of shame, are utterly careless of truth, sacrifice, without any hesitation, the means they use to the ends they serve. . . . The only rule to which the Communist gives unswerving loyalty is the rule that a success gained is a method justified. The result is a corruption both of the mind and heart, which is alike contemptuous of reason and careless of truth."

We must call things by their right names. This is the negation not only of the Christian belief in God and the moral order He has established but also of the Christian estimate of man. The thing that is wanting is reverence for life and respect for personality. Men are treated as instruments of the Cause, as so much State material, rather than as individual human beings made in the image and likeness of God. One is reminded of the reply of Metternich when he was advised that a campaign would take toll of a million lives. "What," he asked, "are a million lives to me?" Under Communism human life is apt to be cheap. A man is liable to find himself without rights which Christianity holds are sacred and inalienable. Look how freedom has been shorn away in Russia. There is no liberty to speak one's mind openly and freely. A citizen cannot start a periodical or write a book or hold a meeting or advocate opinions which, in the judgement of the dictatorship, would threaten the security of the system. Education, art, music, the drama, the radio, science, religion, all the instruments of public opinion, are under government supervision and control. Man has to be the servant, dutiful and submissive, of the State, and the State is omnicompetent and supreme. That is anti-Christian doctrine. It is heresy and must be exposed and opposed.

Yes, we must call things by their right names. There can be no compromise as between Christianity and Communism. They represent diametrically opposed ways of looking at the world and of transforming the world. They are competing with each other for the allegiance of men.

Nevertheless, the Christian attitude to Communism should not be an arrogant attitude. There are evils in Communism, and it is a Christian duty to expose and oppose them, but Christianity is not without its own shortcomings. Too often it is self-contained in its own preoccupations and forgetful of the needs of the world it was commissioned to save. It is taken up with debates about orders and sacraments and ritual and ceremonial and denominationalism when civilization is engaged in a race with catastrophe. It is failing to emphasize with anything like the weight and influence at its disposal that building up military might is not the only way of preventing war, that the best way of combating dictatorship abroad is to extend democracy at home. Communism feeds on hunger, insecurity, injustice, racial discrimination. It makes little appeal to those who know that their rights and liberties are being cared for and nurtured.

The Christian attitude should be an attitude free from malice and hate. There should be no place in it for hysteria or bigotry, the temper which precipitates panicky, ill-advised action. These are days when it behoves Christians more than most citizens to think clearly and speak wisely and with moderation. I quote John Foster Dulles again. "Our Protestant pastors and ministers alone number some 150,000 and they, in turn, can influence millions. Each of these has the duty of self-restraint and also the opportunity to exercise restraining influences on some individual, some newspaper, some politician, who is creating a mood conducive to war. If, during the next few weeks, one million people would each exercise more conscious self-control and do such things as speaking to a friend, writing to an editor, writing to a congressman, the aggregate total effect would be enormous and could make the difference between war and peace."

War will not solve our problems. It never does. It increases misery and deepens confusion. Its results will be the opposite of what the war-minded think can be accomplished. Even a war from which we emerged victorious—if from an atomic war either side emerged at all—would multiply our problems a thousandfold. There would be hunger, despair, anarchy abroad and our free institutions would be weakened at home. War is not the reply to Communism. Communism emerged from the first World War. It was strengthened by the second. It might be supreme in the event of a third. This is not to say that we should capitulate to Russia or cease to resist the expansion of Communism. It is to say that, short of sacrificing Christian principles, we should maintain a conciliatory attitude and keep the door open that may lead to peace. Not long ago I read a statement by the British publisher, Victor Gollancz, who happens to be a Jew, a statement which affords food for reflection. "When Christ told us to do good unto them that despitefully use us and to pray for them that curse us that we may be children of our Father which is in heaven, he was not inventing a method of behaviour which he thought might have satisfactory results: he was making a statement about reality. And every one of us knows in his heart, however bitterly our baser instincts may fight against the knowledge, that the statement is a true one. Evil evokes evil, and good, good; and good, if it is strong enough, overcomes evil."

Finally, the Christian attitude should be a missionary attitude.

Christianity simply must not write off a sixth of the world as irre-trievably lost either to its influence or message. There must be ways of getting through the iron curtain. When the Church was in its infancy it pitched its aim high. It sent its agents to the strategic centres of the world's life—Jerusalem, Antioch, Corinth, Ephesus, Athens, Rome. Paul was never content until he got to Rome. If he were alive to-day, his heart would be set on getting to Moscow. If he had anything to do with the shaping of Christian missionary strategy, it would be slanted in the direction of Africa, Asia, and Eastern Europe, but especially Moscow. We must match the evan-gelistic passion of the Communists. We must pledge ourselves as unreservedly to our cause as they do to theirs. There are six hun-dred and eighty million of us in the world. Is Christianity doing for us what Communism is doing for thousands—giving life a pur-pose, endowing it with feeling, colour, adventure? Are we whole-heartedly committed to it and active in propagating it? A Com-munist is sent into a factory or onto a campus and it is his job to win those with whom he associates. Have you ever tried to win anybody, Communist or otherwise, for Christianity? How else is the Faith to spread?

What Is the Rôle of the Church To-day?

WHAT I have to say to-day was suggested by a member of this congregation. We were talking about the crisis of our time, and the way in which civilization is engaged in a race with catastrophe, and what the Church can do or should be doing to mend matters. It was his opinion that the Church is exerting little direct influence, that it is pretty well on the margin of American life and thought, that it has distressingly few vital relationships, on the one hand, with the working classes, and on the other, with those who are running the United States at the present juncture. The conversation set me thinking, not for the first time, about the rôle of the Church in the crisis which has come upon us.

At the outset let us be clear about one thing. The Church's first business now as always is to be the Church. It exists to turn men's hearts and thoughts and wills toward God and to enable them to see their life and their institutions in the light of God. It exists to inspire prayer and worship and faith and through them to send men and women of character and integrity into the everyday life of the world, men of the stamp of William Ewart Gladstone concerning whom Charles Spurgeon said, "We believe in no man's infallibility but it is restful to be sure of one man's integrity."

This is the primary task to which the Church is called and for which it is specially equipped. It is a task which no other organization is discharging or can discharge. It is an agency for the making and remaking of character. It preaches first and foremost a gospel of moral and spiritual regeneration. It begins, to quote Jesus, with the inside, not the outside of the cup; it begins with the building up of character and then proceeds to the improvement of external conditions. We ought to ask ourselves whether we really think that the work assigned to the Church is less important than that which occupies the attention of politicians. We ought to ask ourselves whether we really think that any solid and stable regeneration of society can be achieved without a new heart and a new spirit.

The first business of the Church now as always is to preach a gospel of moral and spiritual regeneration, but that is not its sole business. It is imperative to change the individual, but it is not enough to change the individual. Something must be done with his environment. Wilberforce recognized that and asked, Shall we rescue individual slaves and leave the slave system intact? J. B. Gough recognized that and asked, Shall we reclaim individual drunkards and never say a word against the liquor traffic? Dr. Fosdick recognized that and from 1919 on kept asking, Shall we pick up the wounded in war and leave the war system intact? Walter Rauschenbusch recognized that and asked, Shall we seek to help the victims of the social order—the badly housed, the unemployed, the underprivileged, those who suffer because of prejudice about their colour or their race—and do nothing to lift the level of the social order itself?

The thing to be borne in mind is that the social order is not entirely made up of individuals now living. It is made up of inherited attitudes which have come down from generation to generation through customs, laws, institutions, and these exist in large measure independently of individuals now living. It is imperative to change the individual. That is the basic principle from which all social reform must spring. It is implicit in the sayings of Jesus: "You must be born again," "Make the tree good and its fruit will be good." In the ultimate analysis changed social conditions are impossible without changed lives. That is the starting-point, but it is only the starting-point. It is imperative to change the individual; it is just as imperative to organize changed individuals into collective action in a wide-scale frontal attack upon social evils with a view to changing the social order.

There are Christians who are apprehensive about this. For them religion is a private matter between a man and his Maker and the business of the Church is seen not as having to do with the patterns and structure of society but with spiritual development and character building. Sir Alfred Zimmern tells of a conversation to which he listened between Baron von Hügel and "the exponent—a very enlightened, public-spirited and devout exponent—of a scheme for the Christianization of a factory of which he was the proprietor." "He enlarged upon the ventilation, the central heating, the welfare system, the part-time education, the dental clinic, the dining room, the swimming pool, the playing-fields,—and all the time the old Baron was growing more and more impatient. Finally he broke in fiercely, 'You haven't begun to understand what Christianity is: Christianity is not refreshment bars and swimming pools; it is a soul in the presence of God.' " Sir Alfred Zimmern adds, "The conversation ended abruptly." But why should it have ended abruptly? The businessman might have replied, "True, religion is first of all a soul in the presence of God, but a soul in the presence of God whom Christ revealed is bound to prove the reality of his religion by his concern for the material needs of those with whom he has to do."

Consider, for example, the field of politics. There are Christians who think that politics ought to be kept strictly apart and distinct from religion and who are averse to any interaction of the one on the other. They are, they say, like oil and water which do not mix. Preachers should keep away completely from political issues and concentrate on the preaching of the Gospel and the saving of men's souls. I remember, being in Britain in the twenties, how when a group of Bishops attempted to bring the Government, the Coal Owners and the Miners together in the hope of ending the disastrous strike of 1926, Stanley Baldwin asked how the Bishops would like it if he referred to the Iron and Steel Federation the revision of the Athanasian Creed. He was generally felt not only to have made a sound point but to have reminded the Bishops of their proper tasks. Nothing could better illustrate the attitude I am describing—the Church and politics in isolation; the Church to be circumscribed in its activity within one area, to concentrate on personal religion, the other areas beyond its scope or influence.

We should never forget the attitude of Hitler and the Nazis in this regard. They insisted that the State had the right to control the whole of man's existence from the cradle to the grave and bade the pastors of the Church confine their attention to otherworldly affairs. The astonishing thing is that so many pastors—there were notable and noble exceptions—accepted the delimitation and never as much as sensed the paganism behind it. A theologian as able and influential as Paul Althaus of the Lutheran Church, during the war years, wrote: "Christianity has neither a political programme, nor any inclination to control or censure political life in the name of Jesus and the Gospels. No Christian law, no Christian standard, exists for the State or for politics. The order of the Kingdom of God is on a different plane from that of the political order. The latter cannot conform to the former." What is that but to declare that the Church has nothing to say about politics, no guidance to offer in the field of national or international policy, no social principles to propound in the name of Jesus and the Gospels? It is precisely the terms, and the only terms, on which the Soviets will make a concordat with the Church or tolerate its existence. See what this means. The Church limited to one field—personal religion. Not a word permitted that appraises or censures political life or state policy either at the national or international levels. The Church obliged to abdicate from an area of action and interest which profoundly affects the well-being, happiness and destiny of millions, and as a result of the abdication, the turning away from the Church of millions because they see that about the things that matter most to them the Church is silent or subservient.

In this country the danger that confronts us lies in the direction of the complete autonomy not so much of a political ethic as of an economic ethic. There are still a surprisingly large number of Christians who hold the view that the Church has nothing to do with the economic order, that its functions are purely spiritual, that it should speak to men about God and prayer and faith, comfort them in their sorrows, provide them with resources for life and for character, but not concern itself with labour-management relationships, or wage levels, or collective bargaining, or the great burning issue of our day, on which hinges the future of civilization, the issue between Communism and Capitalism. But the Church, if it is to be true to its mission, can no more abdicate from the economic than from the political sphere. Its function is primarily spiritual but not solely spiritual, and not spiritual only in the otherworldly sense. The houses men live in, the places where they work, the schools their children attend, the economic order which conditions their lives—ought not these to be the concern of the Church? To have your own house governed honestly, to have it kept clean and wholesome, is a Christian duty. To see to it that your city and your country are honestly governed, and kept clean and wholesome, is a Christian duty too.

This is the teaching of the New Testament. It visualizes Christ as supreme in public as well as in private life. All the provinces of life are provinces in which his authority is to be recognized and his will obeyed. As Studdert-Kennedy put it, "He is lord of the mill as of the minster, and as much concerned with the counting house as he is with the cathedral." The Church is guilty of a dereliction of duty if it does not actively concern itself with all the interests and occupations of men, and in politics and economics Christians should be found serving and honouring him.

I judge that these are things which need to be said to-day. The Protestant Church in particular has been altogether too prone to accept the political and economic limitations which secularizing influences have imposed. It has suffered the world to draw boundaries all round the Christian religion and, for the most part, has been content to retire and remain within those boundaries. In days as critical as these the need is for an advance into the territories from which religion has been expelled—into economics, politics, science, education, art. For the Christian Faith has to do not with a particular province of life but with all its provinces. The sovereignty of God extends not only over prayer and worship but over all our interests and activities. It is the concern of the Church to see the social order and the international order functioning in accordance with God's will. Nothing in the New Testament or in the history of the Church entitles us to regard Christianity as purely a personal affair. So to regard it is to rob it of relevance and practicality. Writes Christopher Dawson, "To keep religion out of public life is to shut it up in a stuffy back drawing room with the aspidistras and the antimacassars when the streets are full of life and youth."

How should religion be brought into public life? There is a marked difference at this point between the Roman Catholic and the Protestant attitudes. The Roman Church is organized deliberately and designedly for political and economic action. From time to time the Pope issues encyclicals which are in the nature of official directives on social issues. The Vatican is a force to be reckoned with politically in the capitals of Europe and in capitals beyond Europe. Throughout its history the Roman Church has done all this as a matter of fixed policy. Protestants, on the other hand, believe that the Church *as an institution* should not aim at the direction of economic and political life inasmuch as it unites its members in a loyalty which transcends the relativities of social action. Protestants urge individual but not institutional participation. They do this from a conviction, corroborated in history, that when the Church enters the political field it finds itself committed not only to relative ends but involved in compromises and expedients inseparable from political action. The history of the Papacy illustrates that whenever the Church has used its power in the political realm it has confused its action with the State and lost its distinctive office as "watchman" above all economic groups and all political parties.

Not institutional but individual participation is the Protestant principle. Christian men and women concerned about the community's housing, sanitation, education, recreation, and because of their concern—not with an eye on the plums of office—going into city councils and state and federal legislatures. Christian men and women active in political parties, labour unions, chambers of commerce. Christian men and women in all walks of life—engineers, teachers, doctors, lawyers, scientists, industrialists—informing, arousing, stimulating the public conscience, intervening in any situation where wrong is being done, lifting up their voice against injustice and corruption, embodying and establishing Christian principles of social action. We Protestants do not identify the Church with any one economic theory or with any political organization, but this does not mean that we have no social or political responsibility. We have to apply the standards of our faith to every department of our conduct. We have to ask ourselves before we vote—not What will best benefit me? but What will be best, in terms of Christian values, for the city, the country? What, for example, does New York City need most just now? The active intervention in its public life of Christian men and women able to command respect by the combination of piety and integrity with outstanding practical ability. From the strong metaphors which Jesus employed to describe the impact of his disciples on society it is clear that he did not envisage a company of men and women content to keep themselves to themselves or to be little groups of pietists. Salt, light, leaven are immensely strong words. They indicate what the rôle of the Church should be.

Dr. E. P. Dickie tells how he once had the experience of attending at the same time to two different sermons. One was preached from the pulpit, and the other from a stained-glass window in which a slight defect had obscured a single letter of the theme, so that it read, "Glory to God in the HIGH ST." There is the rôle of the Church and of the church member—to see to it that the glory of God floods the common life, and all the activities and institutions of men.

With Things as They Are, Why Don't We Rebel?

WITH things as they are, why don't we rebel? That is the question I have been asking myself for a long time. That things are in a bad way goes without saying. Everybody knows that something has gone wrong with our standards of common honesty. We pick up the newspaper and read of policemen working hand in hand with bookmakers and of shameful frauds by men in high positions in handling big government contracts. Wherever we turn—New York, Philadelphia, Chicago, Los Angeles, Washington—it is the same sickening story that confronts us—graft, corruption, the lust for easy money and big money, want of integrity in men in public office.

Men in public office should be above suspicion. We are entitled to expect and demand probity and honesty from them. Why don't we insist on having probity and honesty? It is high time that decent people, who far outnumber the unprincipled ones, rose in protest against what, after all, is not being done in a corner, but is going on right under their eyes. When are the people, the great mass of well-doing and honest people, going to get together in a body and say: "This won't do." We refuse to tolerate such a state of affairs any longer. It has got to come to an end."

All that some of us do is *grumble*. We read the newspaper with its shocking disclosures of unscrupulousness and venality and as soon as we can get anybody to listen we pour out a torrent of complaint. Not long ago a man cut loose on me about city politics and politicians. He worked himself up into a frenzy over the sordid, seamy side of our municipal government. When he had said his say something about him made me inquire whether he had voted at the last election. He had not. That is the trouble with a great many grumblers. All that they do is grumble. They make grumbling a substitute for action. They don't like what is going on but beyond voicing a complaint they do nothing. They shirk responsibility. They play the easy and comfortable rôle of spectators. They don't enter into city politics themselves, or take a hand in the selection of those who do enter into them, or contribute anything like solid, steady support to men of character and principle who are putting up a fight for clean government. There are thousands upon thousands of able and good people in New York who take no active part in the administration of the city's affairs—its housing, its schools, its hospitals, its welfare agencies, its courts, its politics.

Listen to Lewis Gannett describe them as he describes himself. "To an increasing degree we evade our responsibilities as citizens of the city, grumblingly leaving the 'bosses' in control, but we accept no new responsibilities in the country. So the cities remain in the hands of the machines, and the countryside gently loses its inner fibre. We lose something of our moral fibre ourselves. . . . In fact I no longer quite belong either to the country or the city. I accept no deep responsibility anywhere. And there are dangerously many like me in the United States. The tide of city-dwellers flowing to the country has its sinister, irresponsible, isolationist aspects . . . This is a national problem, worth more exploration than it has yet had." Doesn't that bear out what I have been saying? All that some of us do is grumble, and grumbling, when it is a substitute for action, is useless. People who care go and do something.

Some of us don't rebel, and don't even grumble very much, because we are *apathetic*. This is one of the dangers of middle age and of the years that lie beyond it. It is then that men and women are apt to cease to care about what ought to be, are apt to shrug their shoulders over graft and corruption and accept them as inevitable. "We know," they say, "that things are bad, but what can *we* do to alter them?" They become resigned to intolerable conditions just at the very time when they have the reputation and the money and the influence to fight them. They acquiesce in situations against which they should raise their voice and exert their influence in spirited defiance. They don't want to be disturbed. They come to terms with the *status quo* when what is needed is that the *status quo* should be radically altered. They harden themselves and in some cases try to persuade themselves that things are not as bad as they seem, or that it is not their business anyway, or that there is nothing they can do about them. All of which is stuff and nonsense. Things are bad. That they are bad is their business. They can do something about remedying them. The worst thing they can do is to do nothing.

It is as fashionable to be tolerant now as it was to be puritanical a hundred years ago. There is no getting away from the fact that many of our social evils are permitted solely because people have never placed the iniquity of them on their conscience. Through hardness of heart, or self-absorption, or laziness, or sheer unimaginativeness they have never been stabbed into a recognition of the grim realities of the situation. There are evils in this nation's life which could be remedied within a short space of time if the great mass of the people would bestir themselves and organize themselves and say determinedly, "These things shall not be." There is nothing to prevent the carrying out of urgent, over-due reforms to-day except our inertia and apathy. A Swiss writer, Muralt, said a searching thing about the English, which is, however, by no means confined in its application to them. "The great cruelty of the English lies in permitting evil rather than in doing it." Tolerance is a virtue, but there are times when we speak of tolerance and the word we ought to use is apathy. Apathy is not a virtue. It is a positive vice, and is a blood relative of cowardice. It does not look like a very serious evil, but, as a matter of fact, it is one of the most pernicious of evils because it can take such a hold as to be very nearly incurable. It is far easier to save a man from active, open acknowledged sin than to rouse him from the stupor of indifference. When you settle down into apathy, have no concern about social wrong, no zeal for reform you are getting old, whatever your age may be. You are patient when you ought to be impatient. You are cautious when you ought to be rebellious. Tolerance is a virtue but it should never be confused with apathy which is a vice.

Some of us are worse than apathetic. We don't rebel against things as they are because we are *cynical* about them. Graft, greed, exploitation—they are ingrained, we say, in human nature, and human nature can't be changed. They have eaten their way like a cancer into every type of civilized life and they have never yet been eradicated. The dream of righteousness and justice is a beautiful dream but we had better be hard-headed realists, not wishful thinkers or starry-eyed visionaries; Utopia is as far from realization to-day as it ever was. So speaks the cynic. He entertains no hope of remaking the world. He sees no abiding or ultimate cure for the ills of humanity. "The thing that hath been shall be"— that sums up his philosophy. He acknowledges that evil is rife but he has no confidence that anything can be done permanently to eliminate it.

There was turned in to a Commissioner of Investigations in New York a report with this comment: "It may be said that the over-all impression of the philosophy of the Police Department in regard to gambling seems to be that nothing can be done—so why try?" "Nothing can be done—so why try?" That's cynicism. You might just as well leave graft, greed and exploitation alone. If you root them out in one place they will only spring up in another. You needn't get it into your head that a change of rule will mean a change of rulers. Whatever the aims they profess, men and parties always think first of themselves. To some such sombre and cynical standpoint people are constantly capitulating.

> After two thousand years of mass,
> We've got as far as poison gas.

That's cynicism. "The only thing we learn from history is that man never learns anything from history." That's cynicism. "If the war did not make us love our enemies, it at least taught us to hate our allies." That's cynicism. Somerset Maugham wrote a short story called *Rain*. There is an appalling character in the story—a woman, hard as nails, bitter, without principles or morals. Maugham allows her to have the final say. "You men! You filthy, dirty pigs! You're all the same, all of you. Pigs! Pigs!" That's cynicism, cynicism at its worst—incredulous of human goodness, fixing its eye on what is low and cheap and nasty, without faith in God or man. Do you wonder that R. L. Stevenson wrote in his *Inland Voyage*, "I hate cynicism a great deal worse than I do the devil; unless perhaps the two were the same thing"?

And where you have cynicism or apathy you are certain to have to reckon also with *compromise*. In either case, the tendency is to accept things as they are, to come to terms with them, to make the most of them. "What are you in business for?" a college president asked an alumnus. With extraordinary candour the alumnus

replied, "To make my little pile, and then get out." It is an attitude
that is only too prevalent—the acceptance of low standards, values,
ideals; no disposition to alter or amend the *status quo;* instead an
easygoing tolerance and complacency which is undisturbed by it
and not averse to profiting from it.

But where you have apathy, cynicism and compromise you will
also find another nobler temper. The men and women who have
lifted the level of life in their generation have been men and
women who have risen in protest and revolt against evils with
which they were not prepared to temporize or compromise. I
think of Abraham Lincoln standing in a slave market, watching
the iniquitous traffic that there was being transacted, and saying,
beneath his breath: "If ever God gives me the chance, I will hit
this thing, and by God I will hit it hard." I think of Florence
Nightingale furiously discontented with the luxurious conditions
under which she was living, awakening to the world of misery,
suffering and despair which lay outside her little world of ease
and comfort, seeing people eaten up with care, poverty and disease, realizing that her destiny lay among the miserable of the
world, rebelling against the "busy idleness" of a gentlewoman of
means and leisure, and, though it meant a painful break with
her home and with the members of her family who thought she
was demeaning herself and disgracing them, blazing a trail and
for the first time in England making a profession of nursing. I
think of Dick Sheppard writing a rebellious book and calling it
The Impatience of a Parson, a book with hot and blistering sentences in it like these: "I want a disturbance. I want almost anything rather than an unchallenged continuation of these smoth-
ered institutional versions of the fire which Jesus Christ came to
cast upon the earth . . . . Perhaps the thing that worries me most
is that I find those leaders of Christianity who some years ago
I knew to be as fully conscious of the situation as they are more

fully equipped to deal with it than I am, tamed out of recognition, not only by high office, but by the cares and pettiness with which their ecclesiastical life is surrounded. I find them now flying about from committee to committee, so intent on little matters of domestic concern and the defence of a parochial area of religion that I am sometimes forced to wonder whether in their heart of hearts they are not attempting to drown their conscience, which bids them forget denominational loyalties and concentrate on the far vaster issues which confront the very existence of Christianity. Why are these able and good people not more explicitly revolutionary and discontented?"

Thank God for people like Lincoln and Sheppard and Florence Nightingale. Thank God for men and women who have risen in indignation and rebellion against the evils of their day and challenged their contemporaries with the cry:

> Come, my friends,
> 'Tis not too late to seek a newer world.

The world owes much of its progress and the majority of its reforms to them. America needs such men and women now. There is far too much apathy and cynicism and compromise among us. Why are Christian people, by and large, so indifferent to what is going on? Why, in the light of recent disclosures of crime and corruption, is the Church, both Protestant and Catholic, so strangely silent? More than any other institution it should be sensitive to social evil and should resist and oppose it. It is high time that more of its members went into muncipal government and did so from a sense of vocation. It is high time that more of its members were active, as Christians, in the political parties and in the labour unions. It is high time that Christian men and women in all walks of life made it their business, for it is their business, to create a community life that is sound and wholesome, and set themselves not only to enunciate but to establish Christian principles of social action. We need such men and women now—sensitive in conscience, alert in mind, militant in action. The case is trenchantly stated by Christopher Fry:

> Thank God our time is now when wrong
> Rises to face us everywhere,
> Never to leave us till we take
> The longest stride of soul men ever took.
> Affairs are now soul size.
> The enterprise
> Is exploration into God,
> Where no nation's foot has ever trodden yet.
>
>   It takes
> So many thousand years to wake,
> But will you wake for pity's sake,
> Wake up, will you?